UNSHAKEABLE SELF-CONFIDENCE FOR TEENS

OVERCOME SELF-DOUBT, BUILD AN IMPROVED SELF-ESTEEM, AND ACHIEVE EXCELLENCE IN ACADEMICS, RELATIONSHIPS, AND SOCIALLY

MICHELLE OSTAN

CONTENTS

SEEK TO TRANSFORM

INTRODUCTION

I have always been an anxious person. I often felt anxious over minor and trivial things during my teenage years. I was insecure and struggled to open up to the people around me. However, it wasn't a serious or particularly unusual experience to go through as a teenager. Everybody has experienced these emotions to some degree. Besides that, I was just a normal and happy teenager enjoying my young life. I didn't really let anything bother me that much because I always had my family and friends to support me whenever I needed them.

However, there was one period of my life when my mind became a little chaotic because I needed to move away from my hometown and the support I had relied on. My parents decided it would be good for me to go to a private high school instead of a public one, and I agreed. I actually enjoyed my high school years because I got to meet diverse groups of people and made new friends along the way. But reflecting back on it, I realized that I was often overcome by anxiety during those years. I often overanalyzed my circumstances, which fueled my anxiety. I struggled to make wise decisions and became insecure about my abilities and relationships. Worst of all, I started to pay too much attention to how I looked around others. I was so insecure about my appearance that I refused to meet anyone before getting dressed and putting on heavy makeup.

I was so afraid of how people would look at me that I even thought everyone disliked me. I wore a mask to hide the real me because I wasn't confident. I sometimes even felt that I wasn't good enough for anyone because I was scared that people would find me boring and dull. There were instances when I avoided social interactions because I wasn't sure that I'd be able to make an excellent first impression on new people.

The truth is that many teenagers feel this way at some point, and I was one of them. They doubt themselves to the point of severe insecurity. Nowadays, the standards that are upheld in society are even higher. Those who set the standards can't even meet them sometimes. It's ridiculous! Many of you must be on social media, and you've seen celebrities and influencers constantly flaunt their perfect lives. But are they even being truthful? We'll never know. These unrealistic standards are very dangerous. As a teenager, I know that you have so much pressure to always look perfect so that you can impress your friends and new people to gain their validation. This can lead to a lot of mental health issues when you feel the need to put up a perfect and happy façade but refuse to address how you struggle emotionally.

Before we explore more, let's look at some basic ways to overcome self-doubt and improve self-confidence. The most important thing is to do research about your issues. After understanding them, you must try to go beyond your comfort zone because learning to be comfortable in uncomfortable situations is essential to building self-confidence. The following step is to stop giving other people's opinions too much thought. Most of the time, people's opinions don't affect you at all, so why should you care? Comparing yourself to others is also not a good idea because everyone is unique. You shouldn't expect to have the same lives as them. You need to start loving yourself rather than dwelling on self-doubt and insecurity. By accepting who you are and being comfortable in your skin, you'll feel much better overall and become more confident to do whatever it takes to move forward.

Would you also like to know how to get rid of anxiety and insecurity? Answers and proven methods have been made available in this book through my personal experiences, research, and conversations with teens who, after going through their teenage years filled with insecurity, have found themselves and become figures envied by others. Everyone has unique potential, but only very few people use them. It takes a lot of self-confidence to unleash a hidden potential. For instance, you enjoy writing poems but refuse to show them to others because they might ridicule you. Through self-confidence, you'll feel at ease showing off your creation because you don't fear people's reactions. Even if someone criticizes your poems, you can learn from the situation and improve your writing style. This will help you increase your skill and write better poems that others might like.

This book offers various methods to guide you through your difficult teenage years. I've explained how I was very anxious and insecure in my adolescent years, and I overcame these issues after trying so many different methods. In this book, I've compiled the best strategies that helped me to regain my self-confidence. I call them the B.E.S.T. methods, which stands for Being curious, embracing possibilities, and Seeking to Transform. This guide will take you in the right direction so that you can overcome whatever issues you're struggling with.

These methods are essential to follow to tackle self-doubt and establish self-confidence. You'll be provided with insights into the relationship between self-esteem and self-confidence. Some other things you'll learn are how to:

- become more self-aware.
- integrate positive self-talk.
- cope with stress.
- use social media to your advantage.
- transform your mindset.
- deal with peer pressure.
- understand your emotions better.
- learn how to boost your self-confidence.

My favorite self-help books have taught me how to identify negative thinking patterns and given me some powerful tools to fight them. They also made me feel less alone in my thoughts and showed me how normal it is to struggle. Most importantly, they helped me become more self-aware of my anxious thoughts and emotions as well as when and how they were being triggered, which meant I could better manage them. They actually helped me to recognize what was and wasn't normal about my way of thinking. Becoming aware of your own negative thinking patterns and their effects on you (which is like looking at yourself as an outsider) is vital to making positive changes. After all, you can't change what you aren't aware of in the first place!

We might think that only ordinary people like us experience anxiety and insecurity. However, there are many examples of celebrities expressing insecurity and low self-confidence. Let's look at an example from Louis Tomlinson, an ex-member of One Direction. In an interview, Louis mentioned how he was not feeling very confident in the band's first year. He was starting his career in the music industry and was shocked that being in the spotlight could be so difficult. He was constantly compared to his bandmates, and it influenced his faith in himself. Now that the band has been disbanded, Louis has the chance to express himself better and free himself from self-doubt by growing his solo career. Even when he was worshiped by his fans being a member of One Direction, Louis was still feeling inadequate, and only after focusing on the solo projects did he start to find his self-confidence and unleash his potential.

It's possible to become more confident, even when you have to go through the harsh teen years. This book will teach you how to feel better about yourself, which will then help you create stronger relationships with your loved ones, perform better at school, and make new friends along the way. I'm here to guide you to achieve all these goals because I went through the same things as all of you when I was a teenager. I was once filled with anxiety and insecurity, but I overcame them, and you can do the same. However, you need to know that it can be a challenging journey. You'll have to face obstacles to improve your self-confidence and self-esteem, but even though it will be difficult, you should never give up. Focus on your goals and refer to this book for direction.

Now that you know what this book offers, are you ready for the journey to boost your self-confidence? Let's get into it!

BE CURIOUS

1

HAVE YOU LOOKED IN THE MIRROR LATELY?

Have you heard Taylor Swift's song *Anti-Hero*? The song discusses how she tackles her insecurities and low self-esteem. It demonstrates how she sees herself as an anti-hero despite being a hero to her fans. In the song, she explains how she chooses to stare at the sun or anything else instead of the mirror because she's insecure about her appearance. If we look at her, she seems like a perfect woman; she has fame, money, and looks. Why would she feel insecure, right? She's the only one who can see her flaws when everyone else thinks she has everything.

As a celebrity, she's always in the spotlight, so people will always gossip about her. This is the life she needs to accept. By the end of the song, she discovers the root of her problems is inside herself and not others. She believes that all her issues come from her mind. No matter what people say, we shouldn't take them so seriously. People will always talk regardless, so why not just live our lives and control how we view ourselves in our minds?

WHAT IS SELF-ESTEEM ANYWAY?

Jessica was a very cheerful and outgoing teenager who never questioned her looks and had no doubts about what she could be or achieve. Suddenly, her best friend Tina stopped talking to her and avoided her without any explanation. Jessica started questioning herself and finding faults in all she was. She felt like Tina preferred hanging out with other girls because they were prettier, more fashionable, and more outgoing than she ever was. The more she thought about it, the more withdrawn she became and the more self-esteem she lost. She got so consumed by the faults she felt she had that she often lashed out at her other friends. As time went by, she lost more friends because of her attitude. Her performance at school dropped drastically, her relationship with her parents became strained, and she eventually entered depression. This is an example of how bad things can get. Clearly, Jessica needs some help to find herself again.

The Definition and Importance of Self-Esteem

Self-esteem is your own perception of your worth and value and reflects your self-confidence in your skills and qualities (Cherry, 2022c). You should strive for healthy self-esteem because it can affect your mental health, determination, and attitude toward life.

Why is it so important? It helps you make better decisions, create stronger relationships, and improve your mental well-being. Additionally, it'll affect your motivation level since someone with a positive self-view is aware of their abilities and potential, which will lead them to take on new challenges and achieve success. When you have healthy self-esteem, you'll also understand yourself better. You'll find out which areas you are good or bad at. This also makes you become more rational and set realistic expectations for yourself.

Self-doubt is frequently present in people with poor self-esteem. They have a hard time making decisions because they don't trust their judgment. They don't think they can accomplish anything, so they refuse to take action and face challenges. They prefer to get cooped up in their rooms since it's their comfort zone. They have no idea how to strengthen a relationship because they don't know how to express their feelings and needs. In their minds, they can't be loved.

However, having excessive self-esteem is also a bad idea. These people tend to become arrogant because they overestimate their abilities. They're also loud and enjoy boasting about their accomplishments. They think they're perfect, which means they refuse to accept criticism because they don't believe they can make mistakes. They also can't maintain a relationship because all they talk about is themselves instead of listening to others.

How Self-Esteem Is Developed

You might wonder, "How is our self-esteem developed?" Are we born with it? Do our parents, friends, and environment influence it? Many factors are involved in self-esteem development, such as the relationship between the parents and child, coping mechanisms for unfavorable emotions, social behavior, and self-acceptance (Hosogi et al., 2012). Let's explore each of these factors:

- **The parent-child relationship**: The home is the first place in which children build relationships with other people. A positive view of oneself is impacted by how children are treated by their parents (Hosogi et al., 2012). For a child to have healthy self-esteem, parents need to nurture them so that the child can develop physically, emotionally, and mentally.

When your parents nurture you inside and out, you'll grow up feeling secure about yourself. This will also make you gain a more positive outlook in life because they're there to support you. Meanwhile, if one has a parent who lashes out at them at the slightest thing, this severely impacts their self-esteem. When we have a poor view of ourselves at home, it will only be worse outside when we are with strangers.

- **Coping mechanisms for unfavorable emotions**: The way you deal with negative emotions also influences your self-esteem. What do you do when you have negative feelings like jealousy, sadness, or frustration? These emotions hinder us from thinking rationally. You'll be unhappy when you don't know how to cope when feeling them. Looking for healthy coping mechanisms will benefit your self-esteem significantly.

- **Social behavior**: Just like the parent-child relationship, your relationships with your friends and how you interact with people in social settings will also affect your self-esteem. This implies that social skills have an impact on your self-esteem. You can socialize better when you have strong social skills, creating a positive self-view.

- **Self-acceptance**: Those with low self-esteem often hate themselves. Through self-acceptance, you can positively influence your self-view. Self-acceptance helps you embrace every part of yourself, good or bad. Nobody is perfect, so you must accept your flaws. If you focus too much on your weaknesses, you'll just become miserable.

Who Is More Susceptible to Low Self-Esteem?

These days, young girls are the most vulnerable group to suffer from low self-esteem. With the growth of body positivity and gender equality, we think girls will have better self-esteem. Why, then, are young girls more prone to low self-esteem? The reason is because of their brains. According to Harvard Medical School study, female brains are found to have more volume in their frontal and limbic cortices (Goldstein et al., 2001). Researchers believe this can be why women are often less impulsive and more emotionally engaged, and this might explain why we're more likely to be perceptive, empathetic, sensitive, and collaborative (Why Do Young Women, 2022). This also means that the female brain is more active, which makes us worry more. We know the pressure young girls face nowadays; they tend to care about what others think about them. When they can't meet the expectations, they become insecure.

People who have gone through trauma are also more prone to low self-esteem. Trauma survivors, such as sexual abuse, a dysfunctional family, or a life-threatening accident, have a higher chance of suffering from low self-esteem. Before experiencing trauma, these people might have good self-esteem. After the trauma, they're left with insecurity that makes them feel unsure and hopeless.

The Causes of Low Self-Esteem and How to Improve It

You may ask what makes your self-esteem low. Someone's self-esteem is usually built from early childhood. When a person doesn't experience affection and love, they'll feel unlovable. Low self-esteem may also result when someone has experienced trauma or grief. When they feel hurt or pain, negative thoughts surround them. There are also other causes of low self-esteem, such as perfectionism, bullying, mental health problems, etc.

The thing is that it's never too late to change your self-esteem. You still have an opportunity to make it better and get back on track to have a fulfilling life. This way, you may connect back to your life purpose while also strengthening your relationships. How do you change your self-esteem?

- **Being kind to yourself**: You need to start treating yourself better. Sometimes, we forget that we deserve good things and undermine ourselves. Say more encouraging things to yourself first. A positive self-perception will also make you feel better about who you are.
- **Focusing on the positives**: Accepting compliments is a great way to practice this. Rather than thinking that you're not that good, you should start saying thanks when given a compliment. It would be best if you celebrated small achievements; regardless of how small your accomplishment is, you need to be proud of yourself.
- **Establishing a support system**: If you have someone you can trust, you should talk to them about your problems. By opening up to them, they may help you discover solutions. If you're close to any of your family members, they can also become someone who may listen to you.

What Happens When You Don't Take Care of Your Self-Esteem?

I've talked about how important it is to have good self-esteem, but what will happen when you don't develop it? There are a couple of negative side effects of having low self-esteem, and they'll affect different aspects of your life.

People with low self-esteem will have a lack of control. They feel they can't control their lives and prefer to go with the flow instead of taking charge. When a problem appears, they feel powerless to do anything about it. They'd depend on someone else to care for them or ignore the situation entirely, pretending nothing is happening.

These people also regularly compare themselves to others. We know that comparing ourselves to people has a negative effect on our mental health. When someone has low self-esteem, they do this more often. Whenever they see someone better, they feel insecure. Perhaps they envy those with more money, better fashion, or who are more intelligent than them. Rather than working to improve themselves, they'll beat themselves down.

Types of Self-Esteem

According to Henry Tajfel (1982), self-esteem may come from the personal self and social self; the social self is then divided into the relational and collective self. This shows that there are three types of self-esteem:

- **Personal self**: This describes a person's self-view as formed by their individual characteristics and qualities that set them apart from other people (Du et al., 2017). For instance, young girls nowadays are influenced by beauty standards like being slim or having no acne. If a girl doesn't meet these standards because she is not as skinny or has acne, she might think she's ugly and feel bad about herself.

- **Relational self**: It refers to elements of the self-view based on interpersonal relationships, such as with friends or family members (Du et al., 2017). For example, someone from a low-income family might feel bad about their situation if surrounded by rich friends at school.

- **Collective self**: It describes elements of the self that result from being part of social groups, such as an ethnic or a race group (Du et al., 2017). A black student at a school with predominantly white students might feel like a misfit and receive some kind of discrimination from others. This then makes them feel bad about their identity, lowering their self-esteem.

How Self-Esteem Affects a Person's Well-Being

When someone has low self-esteem, they'll be impacted negatively. The effects may include negative emotions like depression, stress, anxiety, etc. Low self-esteem may also lead to relationship issues, such as being scared to leave an abusive boyfriend because you think nobody else would love you. When your relationships with others are bad, you'll have no support system or anyone to talk to. We're all social beings who need to socialize to survive in this world; our well-being and mental health will be harmed if we cannot communicate effectively with them.

WHAT DOES MY SELF-ESTEEM HAVE TO DO WITH SELF-CONFIDENCE?

Before we learn about the relationship between self-esteem and self-confidence, we must first know what confidence is all about. In the simplest definition, self-confidence is trusting yourself. This means having faith in yourself as well as your abilities. This will make you more comfortable with yourself.

Having self-confidence is more crucial than you might think because your entire life can be transformed by it. Let's see some advantages of cultivating self-confidence:

- **It improves motivation**: When you are confident, you'll naturally become more motivated than someone lacking confidence. When someone has low self-confidence, they'll always worry about failing and often decide to avoid taking risks.

- **It increases happiness**: When you have self-confidence, you'll not think twice before taking on new challenges. This means that you have no regrets about missing opportunities presented. When someone has no regrets, they live their life feeling fulfilled.

- **It strengthens relationships**: Confidence helps you to create honest and genuine relationships. You're not worried about impressing people because you're comfortable with yourself. When you show your true self, others will feel that you're someone they connect with on a deeper level.

- **It enhances your self-value**: Through self-confidence, you'll start accepting your flaws. You know that you're not just defined by your weaknesses but also by your abilities. You move forward by focusing on what you can do because you value yourself.

However, if you have low self-confidence, you hesitate to experience new things, thinking they'll turn out bad. You find it challenging to trust people as a result of feeling inferior to them. You'll also become passive in reaching your goals because you think you can't do it. You think you can't achieve anything with your skills, so you choose not to try in order to save yourself from the heartbreak of failing.

The Relationship Between Self-Esteem and Self-Confidence

I've explained about self-esteem and self-confidence, but how are they related to each other? As previously stated, self-esteem is an attitude of appreciating and valuing yourself. Your past experiences and relationships determine your level of self-esteem. However, self-confidence refers to having faith in yourself and changes according to your circumstances. In some situations, people could feel more confident than in other cases. For example, you might feel more confident interacting with people and building relationships than studying.

Although they're different, you need some self-esteem to have the self-confidence to face challenges and take part in activities that make you feel fulfilled. Those with low self-esteem may struggle to feel confident because they don't value themselves. How can someone be confident when they don't even appreciate who they are?

How Low Self-Esteem and Self-Confidence Influence a Person

You're not the only one suffering from low self-esteem and self-confidence. Many people are going through the same situation. While some are only impacted in certain circumstances, others may find it incapacitating because it affects most aspects of their lives. With low self-confidence and self-esteem, you'll discover that bad experiences influence your self-view. This then leads to negative thoughts that discourage you from ever trying again. Instead of learning from your mistakes, you give up easily when something disappointing happens. For instance, if you fail an exam, you'll think you're too stupid to do it anyway and refuse to try again. However, with good self-confidence, you'll assess what went wrong and learn from your mistakes. You don't allow the bad experience to affect your self-view negatively.

Because of low self-esteem and self-confidence, your inner critic is strong. You'll criticize yourself when you feel upset and overwhelmed. This can also significantly worsen your emotional suffering by fueling anxious or irrational thoughts.

What Factors May Influence Your Self-Confidence and Self-Esteem?

Negative experiences may decrease your self-confidence and self-esteem. Perhaps others often bully you about your looks, or you've just broken up with your boyfriend. Additionally, positive experiences like passing an exam or tutoring your friends may increase self-confidence and self-esteem. Everyone has unique experiences in life, so what affects you might not impact others at all. The following are some other experiences that may influence your level of self-confidence and self-esteem:

- performance in school
- social media
- encouragement from loved ones
- body image
- accomplishments and skills

HOW DO I SEE ME FOR ME?

Let's take a look back at Jessica's story. She has to wake up so that she can get the help she needs. Before asking others to help her, she must be self-aware about her attitude. Being ignored by someone who used to be your best friend is not a good feeling, but that doesn't mean you can lash out at friends who still care about you. Through self-awareness, Jessica may see herself more positively and improve her relationships with her other friends rather than focusing on someone who doesn't care about her. This will also help Jessica to be more confident and improve her self-esteem.

If you ever go through the same situation as Jessica, you must look deep within yourself. Do you want to stay friends with someone like Tina? You deserve to have a best friend who cares about you. Be more self-aware and curious about who you truly are to discover your worth. At the beginning of the chapter, I explained Taylor Swift's *Anti-Hero*. She'd rather not look at herself in the mirror because she's scared of who she is. However, you shouldn't be scared of seeing yourself for who you really are. Getting introspective in the mirror is a good thing!

Self-Awareness and Its Importance

Self-awareness is the capacity to observe yourself in an objective manner by reflecting and introspecting (Ackerman, 2021). Do you wish to feel happier and become better at making decisions? Then self-awareness is an essential skill to cultivate. It keeps you focused on becoming the best possible version of yourself. Looking within yourself, you may see your growth and improve things you're not good at. You'll also learn about your strengths and flaws and how they can affect the people around you. This means you can build stronger relationships because you know what you can do for others. You'll also feel more comfortable with yourself because you understand your feelings and values rather than relying on others' opinions.

It's essential to develop your self-awareness. The following are some other benefits of self-awareness:

- **Developing critical thinking**: The capacity for processing and objectively analyzing information is known as critical thinking. Being self-aware allows you to recognize the subjective aspects of yourself, such as your emotions. This way, you'll have better control of your emotions and limit their influence on your thinking process.
- **Improving listening skills**: To create stronger relationships, listening to others is essential. You'll become more empathetic toward others by understanding your emotions and thoughts. This means that you understand that they want to be heard as well, instead of only asking them to listen to you. This also improves your communication skills since you don't miss any information being said.
- **Becoming a better leader**: Are you interested in getting a leadership role at school? Then, it

would help if you were self-aware. A good leader needs to have critical thinking, listening skills, and empathy, which are all the benefits of self-awareness. You'll become more successful in getting a leadership role when you can understand yourself and improve what you're good at.

Self-Awareness and Emotional Intelligence

Emotional intelligence refers to the collection of skills that enable you to identify and control your own emotions (Goleman, 2000). To control your emotions, you'll need to understand them first. How do you understand them? It's through self-awareness. This means that being self-aware increases your emotional intelligence. Emotional intelligence is essential so that you can socialize better with others in society.

HOW DO I IMPROVE MY SELF-AWARENESS?

Let's now learn how to improve it so that you may use it in various aspects of your life. Here are a few methods to practice to build your self-awareness:

Journaling

Through journaling, you may recognize and embrace your thoughts and emotions. It'll lead you to self-discovery, where you may discover your values. Additionally, you may also identify what you don't need. This means you'll focus on the positive things and abandon what's not good for you. Journaling can be done in various ways depending on your preference, such as writing down your feelings and thoughts, drawing your friends and family, or taking pictures of your day-to-day life. By doing this, you'll establish an awareness of your life experiences and memories to build a more optimistic view.

Practicing Meditation

Meditation lets you let go of your negative thoughts by concentrating on your breathing or emotions. By doing this, you'll have the time to look inside yourself without distractions. Nowadays, it's challenging to focus on one thing at a time because we've become swamped. You must, therefore, set aside some time to think about yourself. The best time to do this is in the morning before doing anything else or at night when you're about to sleep. All you need to do is find a quiet place where nobody will bother you, sit down, close your eyes, and let go of the things that worry you. It doesn't need to be long, maybe only 10 to 15 minutes at a time.

Asking for Help from a Trusted Adult or Counselor

If you're finding it difficult to make changes yourself, it's better to ask for help from someone you trust. If you're close to your mom or dad, talk to them about your struggles. At school, you may speak to a trusted counselor to find solutions. The point of developing self-awareness is to have better self-esteem and self-confidence. Don't be afraid to open up to someone who you can trust and won't judge you.

KEY TAKEAWAYS

- Developing healthy self-esteem is important so that you may recognize your values and worth.
- If you have low self-esteem, you can improve it by being kind to yourself, focusing on the positives, and establishing a support system.
- Self-esteem is essential to build self-confidence; those with low self-esteem will have a hard time being confident.
- Self-esteem and self-confidence can be affected by various things, such as our school performance, support system, body image, family situations, and accomplishments.
- Self-awareness plays a role in developing good self-esteem and self-confidence.

- By being self-aware, you'll be able to improve relationships, develop critical thinking, be a better listener, and become a better leader.
- If you wish to increase your emotional intelligence, you must practice self-awareness first.
- Some methods to cultivate self-awareness are journaling, practicing meditation, and seeking help from a trusted individual.

The rest of this book's chapters are ways to learn to be curious about yourself, embrace your imperfections, and transform your self-confidence through activities and relationships.

In Chapter 2, we'll explore more about self-limiting beliefs and self-talk and how this can affect your self-confidence. You'll also learn how to challenge these beliefs and improve your self-talk positively.

2

WHAT DO YOU STAND FOR?

In 2015, a musical was made based on Alexander Hamilton's life. There's one interesting song called *Wait for It* that I'd like to talk about here. The song comments on the differences between Aaron Burr's and Alexander Hamilton's beliefs. It was written from Burr's viewpoint and how he watched as Hamilton became successful and gained influence. Unlike Hamilton, Burr contemplated his misfortunes because he couldn't catch up with the ambitious rival, and he had a legacy to protect, which hindered his way to success.

Burr decided to wait for things to happen because he was sure he would shine later. The thing was that Burr wasn't willing to face the risks and only waited. But because all he did was wait, he often compared himself to Hamilton, which made him jealous. As his resentment toward Hamilton grew, Burr's mind became murderous, and he decided to shoot Hamilton to death.

Misery Loves Company

Alex was always struggling with his math classes. No matter how hard he tried, he couldn't seem to understand anything. He questioned himself, "Why am I not good at math? How come everybody else understands it?" At some point, he started to think that he was incapable of learning new things. Even when he struggled, Alex refused to ask for help because he feared others would laugh at him for being so dumb. He always thought he was a loser because he wasn't good at math. He said to himself, "I'll never be successful or graduate if I can't make any progress." The more he practiced negative self-talk, the more Alex isolated himself from his friends. He felt that he wasn't good enough to be their friend. This also affected his other classes because he focused so much on his failure. In the end, his performance at school worsened, and he was left with nobody to talk to because he distanced himself from others. If Alex could talk to someone, he might identify that his negative self-talk was the only thing limiting his capabilities.

What Is Self-Talk?

Self-talk is your inner voice with which you speak to yourself; this voice creates an internal monologue by fusing conscious thoughts with your beliefs (*Self-Talk*, 2022). Self-talk is essential since it affects your feelings and actions dramatically. Nowadays, we've become more aware of the importance of practicing positive self-talk because it can boost our self-confidence and manage negative emotions. When you can make positive self-talk a habit, you'll have better self-esteem and become more motivated in life. When problems appear, you'll concentrate on finding a solution rather than blaming yourself or talking poorly about yourself.

How Does It Work?

For some, it's easy to practice positive self-talk. However, others find it difficult because they're used to letting negative thoughts in. To master positive self-talk, you should allow negative feelings to leave first. When you concentrate on good thoughts, positive self-talk becomes more natural through practice. Self-talk isn't only positive though. There is also rumination or negative self-talk. Self-talk can be uplifting or upsetting, and it relies on your personality. If you're an optimist, you'll typically have more positive self-talk. However, you'll tend to practice negative self-talk if you're a pessimist.

In positive self-talk, you'll encourage yourself through happy thoughts. Before turning positive self-talk into a habit, you must recognize when negative thoughts enter your mind and then transform them into positive ones. The following are some examples of positive self-talk to practice:

- "I'm pretty sure I'll pass the writing test since I've studied so much."
- "I'm proud of myself for going this far."
- "I'm beautiful, so I'll wear whatever I want."

In rumination, your inner voice will turn negative because your mind focuses on bad feelings, which lowers your self-esteem. Sometimes, it might make you refuse to try because of an irrational fear of failing. Here are several instances of negative self-talk:

- "I'm too ugly to be liked by anyone in this world."
- "I failed to pass the test. I'll never be successful."
- "I'm so overweight, I don't think any of my effort for weight loss will make a difference."

How Positive Self-Talk Affects Your Self-Confidence and Performance

Positive self-talk is like having a motivational speaker in your mind. Rather than expecting someone else to motivate you, you use your thoughts. You should tell yourself things that will help you develop a better self-view. This way, you may boost self-confidence while getting rid of your insecurity. Consider how you talk to your loved ones. Do you criticize or scold them for every mistake they make? Probably not. It would be best if you encouraged them so that they can get up and try again. Often, we encourage the people around us without realizing that we let our negative self-talk creep in.

Through positive self-talk, you also become better at managing stress. This means you'll feel more in control of your emotions and thoughts. When you start taking charge, you become more productive and effective. For instance, you're given a difficult assignment. Instead of stressing out, positive self-talk will convince you to trust your abilities. This helps you to relax and focus on finishing the task. Your performance will improve significantly when you avoid concentrating on the negatives.

How Negative Self-Talk Affects Your Self-Confidence and Performance

Negative self-talk can have some severe consequences. Negative thinking will make you lose motivation and leave you feeling hopeless. People who constantly criticize themselves also experience more stress because they believe they can't change their situations. They focus on the worst-case scenario, even though it hasn't happened. Negative self-talk makes you pass on opportunities because you're scared. Your worries will lower your confidence and hinder you from achieving your goals because your mind thinks you can't do it.

This will also lead you to become a perfectionist. You make yourself believe everything has to be perfect; if it's not, you're a failure. This then makes you more stressed because your mind always works to fix things. For example, if you received 90% instead of 100% on your exam, you'll blame yourself for not getting the perfect score. When you focus too much on this, you'll spend your time sulking and have no time to study for other exams, which means your future performance may suffer.

The Issue with Self-Pity

When life gets difficult, you may have pitied yourself for the bad things that happened. When you are focused on your problems and feel sorry for yourself, that is known as self-pity. It can lead to being obsessed with your problems and tends to drive people away and make both you and them miserable. I once had a friend who lost her mom at an early age. It was a tremendous loss for her family because she was still young when it happened. Then, 15 years later, she would still blame her struggles on her mom's death and would take days to sulk. This made people distance themselves from her, and she got more depressed over the event. When you're constantly feeling sorry for yourself, you won't be able to enjoy your life because becoming too wrapped up in the negatives of life makes you unhappy. Self-pity makes you believe there's no point in finding solutions to your problems because you think nothing seems to go according to plan. The problem is that encouraging words from your loved ones may not even help you from self-pity unless you decide to stop feeling sorry for yourself.

Self-Pity Can Act as a Validation

Self-pity may come from stress, but this isn't always the case. Occasionally, self-pity can mask a need for validation. The need for validation may indicate that you believe that you deserve the situation you face. For instance, if anything bad occurs, you think you deserve it because of something you did. Let's say you've just failed to win a competition; you blamed yourself and talked to others about it, and they sympathized with you. When others respond sympathetically to your situation, it'll support your negative validation (Gillette, 2021). This is an external validation when you get attention from the people around you.

Self-pity can be Addictive.

Do you know that self-pity can be addictive? Nowadays, the media shows us how easy it is to have a victim mentality. It makes us believe we are too powerless over our lives and situations. Honestly, I understand how many people pity themselves because it's much easier than facing problems. You may ask, "Why is it me that has to experience this misfortune?" This type of question will only make you dwell in your self-pity. I know that it can be tempting to stay sad. It's like a drug that makes you addicted. However, to get out of self-pity, you must face the challenges to create positive transformations in life.

How Negative Self-Talk and Self-Pity Shape Your Beliefs About Yourself and Impact Your Development

When you dwell on negative self-talk and self-pity, you'll focus on the bad situation instead of moving forward. When you concentrate on negativity, you can't embrace life to the fullest. You'll end up beating yourself down and living in misery. You'll always see yourself in a negative light. You believe nothing good will ever happen to you because it's your destiny. You can't see that there are still good things happening because you're too preoccupied with the pain.

Negative self-talk and self-pity also hinder your development in relationships. You become self-absorbed and ignore others. For instance, you've just broken up with your girlfriend and decided to isolate yourself from your friends. This will create a distance between you because they may think you only care about your ex and not them. It would be best to spend time caring for other people's needs and emotions to develop stronger relationships. However, if you always focus on your painful experiences, others will have no importance in your mind. When this happens, you might even ruin your relationships, and others may choose to stay away from you.

DO I REALLY BECOME WHAT I THINK?

In this section, we'll learn and talk about self-concept. Self-concept is your perception of yourself, but it's also affected by your loved ones and the people around you (Cherry, 2022b). It can also be defined as the way you view your actions, skills, and unique traits. For instance, you might see yourself as a good kid since you're always there to support your family. Self-concept is an important part of yourself because it influences your behavior and motivation. It also impacts your perception of who you believe yourself to be and your self-worth.

The Three Parts of Self-Concept

Carl Rogers, a psychologist, created one of the most well-known foundations for self-concept, believing it should be divided into three main parts (Gillette, 2022). The following are the explanations:

- **Self-esteem** refers to how you see your value and worth. It's also affected by different factors, such as how you see yourself around people and how they see you. For instance, you're proud of yourself for being a kind person.
- **Self-image or real self**: This is the way you actually perceive yourself. It's influenced by a variety of factors, including the way you look and how you act. For instance, you see yourself as a good friend to your classmates.
- **Ideal self**: This is the part that refers to the vision and goals of who you wish to become. It's an image that appears if everything goes according to your plan. Your ideal self will have

the qualities you strive to cultivate. For example, you wish to become a kind person who is liked by everyone.

Incongruence and Congruence

Above, I've explained your ideal self and real self. Incongruence happens when there's a difference between the person you want to be and how you currently perceive yourself, and it causes low self-esteem (Cherry, 2022b). Conversely, congruence occurs when your ideal self and real self overlap or are the same. However, in reality, humans are never satisfied with the way they perceive themselves. We always want to change various things. Many of us are looking to have congruence between our ideal self and real self, and if we aren't, we might suffer from negative emotions, stress, and anxiety.

How Does Our Self-Concept Develop?

Your self-concept starts to form in your childhood and develops as you get older. In part, it changes through how you interact with others. As you grow up, you'll experience various roles. When you succeed in something, you'll value yourself more in that area and create a self-concept based on it. When you get more accomplishments, you'll have a more positive self-concept. For instance, if you're good at math and you get praised by your teachers, this will make you feel good about yourself and have a better self-perception.

What Distinguishes Self-Concept From Self-Esteem?

You may think self-concept and self-esteem are the same, but they're not. Self-concept refers to the general description of yourself. You might say that you're a great writer or an exceptional athlete. Meanwhile, self-esteem is your assessment and view you may have about yourself. You may say you feel proud of yourself for being a great writer or athlete. In other words, self-concept provides an answer about who you are, and self-esteem gives one about how you feel about yourself.

Your Reality Is the Outcome of Your Thoughts

Many people disagree that how we think will create our reality. They believe it's blaming the victims even when they haven't done anything wrong or that nobody wants anything negative to happen in their lives. In this regard, I agree with them because nobody actually wishes to experience something bad. However, we also create our reality because there are things that we can control, and if we refuse to admit it, we deny that we have this power.

Even though there are things we can control, I know

some things are out of our control as well. Let's explore these more.

The things that you have no control over in life are unexpected circumstances. For instance, someone's death, the family you're born into, accidents, etc. These situations can make someone anxious, and sometimes, they might get stuck in them. They're drowning in what has occurred and scared that they'll experience it again. It would be best to let go of what you can't control and focus on the present to become more reliable and connected to others.

You also influence others with your actions. For instance, your friend decides to open up to you about getting pregnant. Your response to this news will affect her reaction to you. If you choose to blame her for her mistake and belittle her, she might retaliate by slapping you. You may not anticipate this reaction because you think that it's her fault for getting pregnant in the first place. However, if you respond with more compassion by listening to her and helping her search for solutions, she'll appreciate your support.

As for the things you can control, these are the ones that help you create your reality. This is how you perceive the events that happen to you. This perception will determine your emotions and how you react. Nobody can decide what you think and how you act. It all depends on you. As an example, your significant other decides to break up with you. If you think, "I'm so ugly; that's why he broke up with me," you'll dwell on negative feelings and stress. However, if your mind says, "I'm glad I dodged a bullet because he was only using me," you can move on faster. This is how you choose what you want to think, which in turn will determine how you act and feel.

A thought might not be true initially, but if you keep repeating it, it'll eventually become a belief. This is why you must filter and take charge of your thoughts so that your reality becomes more positive.

How Does the Brain Filter What People Say About You?

Our brains have a selective filtering system called priming that makes them look for something backed up by a particular belief (Vilhauer, 2020). As a result, it might be challenging to see proof that contradicts an established belief in your mind. Your brain establishes your own truth, and that's why you think your perception of the world is true. After going through this filter, you'll create your self-concept. This consists of who you are in the present and what you can become in the future. If you keep bad thoughts by thinking you're unlovable, your self-concept becomes negative. However, if you believe you're capable and clever, you'll have a better self-view that creates a healthy self-concept and self-esteem.

How Do Your Thoughts Affect Your Self-Concept?

The saying "you are what you think" has probably crossed your mind before. The way you think about yourself will shape your self-concept. How far you're willing to go beyond your comfort zone to fix an issue or accomplish a dream depends on how healthy your self-concept is. To have good beliefs and self-esteem, you must have a healthy self-concept first, and it all starts in your mind. This positive self-concept influences how you question yourself, communicate and socialize with others, and perceive your surroundings. You see how essential having a healthy self-concept is, and because it begins with your thoughts, you have to fill your mind with positive things. For example, you have a crush on a boy, but he's decided to date your friend. If you think he chooses her because she's prettier and you're too ugly, you'll have a negative self-concept. This will affect your friendship with your friend. However, suppose you think they're together because they're a better match, and there are still many other boys to date. In that case, you won't question your appearance.

DO YOU ACCEPT THE CHALLENGE?

Similar to Aaron Burr's experience, self-limiting beliefs might lead people to make decisions they'll regret later. Burr believed that Hamilton had everything he wanted, making him jealous. He couldn't stand the fact that Hamilton became more successful than him, even though all he did was wait. Rather than acting to change his situation, Burr dwells on his negative self-talk and self-limiting beliefs. This made him stick with his negative thoughts, and he eventually murdered Hamilton. As with Alex's story, he was also struggling with these issues. When he couldn't learn math as fast as his classmates, he thought that he was incapable of learning new things.

These two people couldn't overcome their struggles and surrendered to their negative thoughts. However, they could've tried transforming their self-concepts by challenging their negative self-talk and self-limiting beliefs. When you can recognize these in your life and then take action to challenge them, you'll improve your self-concept and self-esteem. The reality is that it all depends on you if you wish to change your life.

How to Overcome Negative Self-Talk and Self-Limiting Beliefs

Before you can overcome negative self-talk and self-limiting beliefs, there are a couple of things you need to do first. To get started, you must practice positive self-talk, find the antidotes to self-pity, and stop negative thoughts. Would you like to know more about these?

Practicing positive self-talk is very helpful if you want to feel better about yourself. Learning to change your inner voice to be more motivating if you tend to be negative is possible. Creating a new habit requires effort, but your self-talk may change as you practice. How do you do this?

- **Recognize the pitfalls of negative self-talk**: Some situations can make you doubt yourself, leading to negative self-talk. For instance, group projects make you insecure, especially if you must work with ambitious students. When you identify these situations, you can prepare yourself and avoid negative self-talk.
- **Spend time with positive friends**: You'll pick up on the attitudes and feelings of those around you. When the people surrounding you are positive, you'll also become like them. However,

you might pick up their characteristics if they're toxic and enjoy bullying others.

- **Find the humor**: Your stress and anxiety can be reduced simply by laughing. You can find ways to smile and laugh by joking with your friends or watching funny videos on your phone.

The next thing we'll explore is the antidote to self-pity. If you want to get rid of self-pity, you need self-awareness. By being self-aware, you can snap out of self-pity as it appears and focus on a healthy mindset.

- **Change your perspective**: When you focus too much on your problems, you may think others have it easy. We all know that it's not true because everyone has their issues. You're not the only one with obstacles, so if others can overcome them, why can't you?
- **Practice gratitude**: Being grateful helps you focus on the positives. This also allows you to feel more content with your life. There are many things to be thankful for, no matter how small they are, such as having good parents or people who care about you, enjoying a homecooked meal, or even making it through a tough time in your life.

- **Ask others for solutions**: Self-pity can make you feel alone and drive others to distance themselves from you. Why don't you ask them for solutions instead of telling others how you blame yourself for your problems? For instance, if you're struggling in English class, instead of putting yourself down, you can ask for help from your friends. Perhaps you can ask for tutoring sessions to follow the class better.

Challenging negative thoughts is the last method to overcome negative self-talk and self-limiting beliefs. This approach is more than just thinking positively because you need to put in more effort. How do you challenge negative thoughts?

- **Question the thought**: Searching for proof that contradicts the unfavorable thought you're feeling can be beneficial. For example, if you ever think, "I'm terrible at singing," consider whether any proof says otherwise. Has your friends or family ever complimented you for your singing?

- **Practice self-love**: You need to be compassionate to yourself. You must try to love yourself before others can love you. When you show love and appreciate yourself, you'll reduce negative self-talk.

WORKSHEET TO CHALLENGE NEGATIVE THOUGHTS

Irrational negative thoughts can result in poor self-esteem, low self-confidence, and a negative self-concept. Even if you always get praised for being smart by your teachers, one nasty comment from your friend might make you feel horrible. If you're someone who cares so much about your performance at school, one criticism will lead to irrational fear and dictate how you feel about yourself. According to Judith S. Beck (2011), before questioning your abilities when you receive criticism, you need to challenge negative thoughts first by answering these questions:

Question	Answer
Does my thought have any solid proof?	
Does my thought conflict with any other evidence?	
What would my friends or parents say in this situation?	
Will this situation affect me next month? What about next year?	
Can I change the situation if I look at it from a positive perspective?	

After answering these questions, what revelation did you find? Were your negative views valid in any way? Or were they just irrational? Most probably, they weren't as bad as you thought once you looked at them from a different perspective.

KEY TAKEAWAYS

- Self-talk is your inner voice. When you motivate yourself, it means that you have positive self-talk. However, if you only focus on negative thoughts, it shows that you have negative self-talk.

- Self-pity happens when you feel sorry for yourself. It can be dangerous, though, because it can make you look for external validation, and it's easy to become addicted to having a victim mentality.
- Self-concept is your perception of yourself and is divided into three parts: your ideal self, real self, and self-esteem.
- Incongruence means that there are differences between your ideal self and real self, while congruence refers to the overlap between the two.
- Even though you have no control over some things, you do have control over many other things. It depends on whether you use the power or not.
- To overcome negative self-talk and self-limiting beliefs, you have to practice positive self-talk, discover the antidotes to self-pity, and challenge negative thoughts as they appear.

When it comes to stress and other mental health issues, the types of coping mechanisms that you have are crucial. In Chapter 3, you'll find out how to build healthy coping mechanisms so that you may cope better.

3

WHEN IT'S TOO MUCH TO HANDLE

The younger generation is becoming aware that talking about mental health issues is important. They are more open about their struggles and raising awareness so that society can be more accepting of those struggling to help people come forward.

Nowadays, teen celebrities are also opening up about their issues. You might think they have perfect lives because they have money, looks, and fame. From our eyes, they have everything, and everyone wants to be like them. You don't realize that being a celebrity has so much pressure. They have to be in the public eye 24/7, and their lives are constantly being scrutinized. Imagine having no privacy because people want to know what you eat, who you date, and how your family is. That's the price of fame.

There are times when the pressure can become too much, affecting their mental health. This is when they need to make wise decisions and choose coping mechanisms to deal with it. But we all know that being under pressure may cloud our judgment. Many of these teen celebrities fall into depression, low self-esteem, and drug abuse. For example, Justin Bieber decided to cancel several dates of his *Purpose* tour because he felt depressed and alone (Valenti, 2019). Justin also explained how he had abused prescription drugs before because he couldn't handle the nature of his work. He mentioned that drug abuse caused his life to become dark and made him worse.

Justin's story shows that the way he coped with stress was unhealthy. Suppose you wish to feel better under stress and pressure. In that case, you must find healthy ways to deal with them because your chosen coping mechanisms are essential in improving your mental health.

AM I ALLOWED TO FEEL STRESSED?

All Becky wanted was to go through her high school life in peace so she could graduate and go to university. However, as a teenage girl, she faced much pressure from other girls to fit in. She tried to stay away from them, but she also felt the need to socialize so that she could have friends. In school, there were some strange standards to follow to be respected, such as wearing clothes or makeup from certain brands. She knew that she wasn't forced to do all those things, but she would look cool and cute when she followed them.

As if peer pressure wasn't enough, Becky also had to handle her parents' high expectations. Her parents wanted her to always get good grades while participating in extracurricular activities. She had to keep up because she didn't want to disappoint them. This put Becky under tons of stress. She tried to juggle her school and social life and had no time for herself. Since she had no idea how to manage her stress healthily, her performance at school spiraled down. It caused her burnout; her relationships with her friends and parents were getting worse because she didn't know how to set boundaries, and the whole thing made her self-esteem and self-confidence plummet.

What Is Stress, How Does It Work, and How Is It Diagnosed?

Stress refers to the shift that creates strain on your body, mind, and emotions, and it's your body's reaction to anything that demands your focus and attention (Scott, 2022). Your body adjusts to new surroundings with the assistance of stress reactions. Stress may help you stay awake, driven, and prepared to escape danger.

For instance, if you're about to do an important presentation, your stress may make you work more or stay late to prepare for it.

Then, how does stress work? When stress happens, your nervous system will change your breathing, heart rate, and vision (*Stress*, 2021). Stress can make you irritated, scared, and frustrated. Physically, you might feel so tired and burned out that you can't handle it anymore. Often, stress is not easy to identify and see. It might occasionally be caused by a clear source, but slight day-to-day pressure from your friends, family, or school often harms your well-being (Scott, 2022). In reality, stress is normal, and everyone experiences it. It's how they respond to and deal with it that differs from person to person.

Because stress is a response to new situations, you can't really measure it, and it's different from one person to another. Nobody else except yourself can tell how much stress you are under. If you go to a medical professional, they may also ask you some questions to assess if you're experiencing stress or not. Severe stress can also manifest to affect your physical health. For instance, you could have high blood pressure because of stress (*Stress*, 2021). People also feel stress differently; for example, you might feel overwhelmed when you have to do three assignments daily, but your classmates might feel fine because they enjoy it.

Types of Stress

You may think all types of stress are negative and bad, but that's false. There's positive stress called eustress. This is what they call exciting stress because it's the healthy amount of stress that drives you to take on new challenges, which are connected to adrenaline spikes (Scott, 2022). Eustress takes you beyond your comfort zone while helping you overcome challenges like going on a first date. For example, going on a first date lets you get to know the other person and build a new relationship. The other type is distress, which is the stress that makes you feel pressured and burdened because your attitude, mood, and sleep can be negatively affected and disturbed (Segal et al., 2023). This may also cause mental health problems like depression because you're experiencing more stress than you can bear and deal with. For instance, you don't have enough money to buy a new school uniform, or you're going through treatments to recover from an illness.

How Does Stress Influence Your Body and Mind?

When you feel stressed out, many symptoms may appear, whether physically or mentally. However, these symptoms are hard to notice sometimes. Stress may creep in when you're vulnerable. For example, stress may come when trying to finish many assignments simultaneously. Still, you don't notice it because you're too focused. You may even get used to it and think that constantly stressed out is normal. When you don't recognize stress symptoms and work to overcome them, they'll affect you negatively and create mental health issues. Here are some of the effects of stress:

- Physical effects: Weak immune system, rapid heart rate, stomach problems, tiredness, dizziness, high blood pressure, sleeping problems, etc.
- Mental effects: Irritability, panic attacks, sadness, anger, unhappiness, depression, mood swings, loneliness, and so on.
- Stress can be temporary or prolonged depending on the situation that leads to it. For instance, if your stress is caused by an upcoming exam, it may end once you've completed it. However, if the reason is that you disagree with your parents' divorce, it may last until you can accept and make peace with it.

How Much Stress Is Too Much?

Since stress can have negative effects, knowing your personal limits is crucial. How much stress someone can handle will vary. Some people can stand their ground and stay calm during stressful situations, while others tend to break down when faced with minor difficulties. Some individuals even thrive on the thrill of stressful lives. Moreover, your capacity for handling stress is also affected by the following factors:

- **Support network**: When you have a strong support network, you may lower your stress level. If you're under pressure, your loved ones can be there to give you encouragement. For instance, if you fight with your parents at home, you may talk to your friends about it. They become someone to depend on, so you don't have to face it alone.

- **Positive outlook**: Your capacity to deal with stress depends on how you view life and its inescapable difficulties. When your perspective is positive, you won't dwell so much on your problems and can move forward. For example, suppose you fail to win a math competition instead of stressing out and blaming yourself. In that case, your positive outlook helps you to learn from your mistakes.

- **The ability to control emotions**: If you don't know how to control and handle your emotions, you'll become more vulnerable to anxiety and stress. Recognizing and managing your emotions might help you cope with stress better and recover from setbacks. For instance, you just got rejected by your crush, making you feel sad and angry. Rather than getting upset and insulting your crush, you should step back and manage your emotions because you're not entitled to a relationship just because you like someone.

What Causes Your Stress?

Many things can cause stress, especially in this modern world. As I've said before, one situation can stress someone but not others, and the most important thing is how you choose to handle it. Before you take steps to deal with stress, you should be aware of when you're stressed and identify the source. The following are some common causes of stress:

- **Stress at school**: It's common to experience stress at school occasionally. However, too much stress can hurt your performance and mental well-being. Your success at school can also be determined by it.
- **Financial stress**: As a teenager, you might not have to worry about working or earning money. However, suppose you're in a family

with unstable financial conditions. In that case, you may also worry about insufficient money to eat or buy school supplies.

- **Loss and grief**: The loss of a loved one might be the biggest life challenge to go through. The pain of losing someone may feel unbearable, and that's why people often feel extreme guilt, sadness, and shock.

WHAT DO YOU DO WHEN YOU'RE STRESSED?

When you feel stressed or encounter a stressor, you automatically rely on actions or behaviors that can help you cope, called coping mechanisms. What are coping mechanisms? They are your go-to patterns and actions when faced with particularly stressful circumstances that you frequently rely on to maintain your composure as you get used to shifting situations (Cooks-Campbell, 2022). To understand the stressors and methods for coping mechanisms, let's explore more about them.

Internal and External Stressors

Stress can come from different sources (or stressors). All stress indeed causes your mind and body to respond, but it's still essential to identify the stressor so that you can know how best to cope. Internal stressors are what you think and feel that can make you get stressed out or anxious (Maddock, 2023). Several examples of internal stressors are unrealistic expectations, insecurities, personal goals, and perfectionism. Meanwhile, external stressors are circumstances you have no control over that cause a stress reaction (Maddock, 2023). Some external stressors include an upcoming test, a severe illness, relationship issues, and family problems.

Approaches for Coping

According to Sukhman Rekhi (2023), there are two approaches that we usually use to cope with stressful situations: the cognitive approach and the behavioral approach. To make it easier, I'd like to use an example to explain them. Let's say you're very busy with assignments and forget your best friend's birthday. You set a reminder on your phone but forgot about it and decided to turn off your phone the entire day to finish your homework. You remembered the birthday the next morning, and when you saw your best friend, they looked upset and disappointed. You felt bad for missing their birthday and disappointing them. Sadly, you can't travel back in time. What would you do to deal with this unpleasant situation?

- The cognitive approach involves thinking (Rekhi, 2023). In this situation, you might want to blame yourself for missing the birthday and believe that you're a terrible friend. This will not help you in any way and will only make you feel worse. What you need to do is learn from the mistake and better yourself. It would be best if you forgave yourself first.

- The behavioral approach is based on action (Rekhi, 2023). After forgiving yourself, you need to approach your best friend and apologize. You must find ways to repair the friendship. Maybe you get them a big present to make up for missing their birthday or offer to treat them to a meal. You should listen to what they want and make it a reality.

Coping Mechanism Methods

We can never get rid of stressors in our lives, but we may still try to deal with stress with various healthy methods. Here are the two coping mechanisms you can consider using to handle stressful situations. Problem-focused coping involves seeking help or trying to ease the stressful situation. In contrast, emotion-focused coping aims to control the emotional distress that appears in reaction to it (Cooks-Campbell, 2022).

Let's take a look at an illustration to understand these coping mechanism methods. You just found out you failed a class, making you feel terrible. You're scared of telling your parents because they might be disappointed in you. With problem-focused coping, you'll let your parents know and tell them what you plan to do to improve. For example, you'll spend more time studying and less time playing games, or you may ask a classmate to tutor you. With emotion-focused coping, you decide to sit quietly after receiving the news. You feel too stressed out to address the situation, so you choose to walk to the park for some peace. You know that if you talk about it now, you'll lash out and cry.

Mechanism Styles

When faced with stressful circumstances, everyone reacts differently. Some would be motivated to solve the issue immediately, and others might prefer to avoid it altogether. There's no right or wrong way to cope because it depends on what you're comfortable with. However, it's still essential to understand the various styles of coping mechanisms.

The first style is the active coping mechanism, and it deals with the issue at hand immediately (Scott, 2022). By doing this, you're trying to lessen the effect that the stressor has on you. For instance, your boyfriend is angry at you. With this style, you'll ask him to talk through the problems so that you can resolve them right away. The second style is the avoidance coping mechanism, which involves avoiding stressful situations instead of addressing them directly (Scott, 2022). For example, you have a challenging assignment that is stressing you out. Rather than trying to finish it, you avoid looking at it by procrastinating. But you know you'll not stop thinking or stressing about the assignment unless you get it done.

Mechanism Types

Not every way to cope is good because some might even be dangerous for you. By using adaptive coping mechanisms, you can alter a stressful circumstance to be more positive or adapt how you respond to stress (Bailey, 2022). Some examples of adaptive coping mechanisms are as follows:

- writing in a diary
- working out at the gym
- reading new books
- venting to a friend

Meanwhile, maladaptive coping mechanisms refer to negative coping methods, which are often the default response of those who've gone through trauma or abuse (Bailey, 2022). Because these coping skills are negative, they'll have damaging effects on your body and mind. The following are some examples to avoid:

- drug abuse
- suicidal thoughts
- alcoholism
- binge eating

Everyone has their own coping mechanism, whether it's reading a book, venting to a friend, or other types like binging or substance abuse. However, if you find it too much to handle, it's time to ask for help from a trusted individual.

TURNING A NEW LEAF

From Justin Bieber's story, you can see that his coping methods were negative (or maladaptive) because he resorted to drugs to feel better. However, he realized that it made him worse and that he needed to escape those habits. In the end, Justin decided to sober up and take time away from the spotlight. Now that he's married to Hailey Bieber, Justin's life looks so much better than when he was coping with prescription drugs. How about you? What are your coping mechanisms? Are they adaptive or maladaptive? If you find that your coping mechanisms are harmful, it's time to break the cycle. You might think you feel better using maladaptive coping mechanisms, but they'll make you worse in the long run. Let's learn how to change your maladaptive coping mechanisms to healthy ones:

- **Distraction**: When your mind turns to negative thoughts, diverting your attention from them is essential. You can find a distraction by filling your day with positive activities. You're free to choose what you enjoy, such as doing sports, spending time with friends, or taking a walk in a park.

- **Self-compassion**: When negative thoughts enter your mind, you might want to shame or blame yourself. However, this isn't a good idea because you'll feel worse. Instead, you should show self-compassion to feel more confident and have better self-esteem. You may write yourself a letter of self-compassion where you can alter your self-perception by picturing how worthless you feel and viewing it with love and compassion (Sutton, 2020).

- **Meditation**: Meditation is an excellent way to break maladaptive coping patterns because it offers you the chance to spend time with yourself. During this time, you'll become more imaginative, creative, and focused, which will help you balance your life. Additionally, meditation helps you focus on one thing at a time to distract your mind from stressful or worrisome situations. For example, as you wake up in the morning, you may set aside 5 to 10 minutes sitting in bed to meditate. You can choose one happy memory or situation to think about and focus on it. This way, you'll create a more positive attitude to go through your day.

HEALTHY COPING MECHANISMS

Do you think your life is getting more complicated and busier because of your school schedule, assignments, or family expectations? If so, paying attention to your emotional well-being is still important. As you go through life, it's normal to feel stress, which is why finding healthy ways to cope with it is essential. The following are several activities to consider as your coping mechanisms.

- **Exercise**: Exercise causes the release of endorphins, which function as natural painkillers and mood enhancers (Hodge, 2023). After you exercise, you'll feel happier and have better concentration. You can start small because you don't have to start big by going to the gym to do heavy weightlifting. For instance, maybe you may begin with a 15-minute walk every day and increase the time once you get used to it. You can also join extracurricular activities at school, such as volleyball or basketball.

- **Explore your creativity**: Creative activities will allow you to express your emotions through something real, which helps to make sense of your experiences. For example, you can write poems, paint landscapes, or play musical instruments. Whatever activity you choose will help you get a sense of achievement because you're able to do something by yourself. These activities will also allow you to divert your worry from negative thoughts to something fun and exciting.

- **Build a support system**: When you have a support system, you'll have friends to listen to you and give you solutions. If you face challenges, they'll be there to navigate and overcome them. This will improve your ability to cope with stress since you always have someone by your side. There are many methods for getting social support, such as getting in contact with your family members, spending more time with your friends, joining an online support group, or getting involved in school activities.

KEY TAKEAWAYS

- Stress happens when there's a change that causes physical and mental reactions and may come from daily pressures, like family or social expectations.
- Stress is divided into eustress, which is exciting and fun stress, and distress, which is overwhelming and negative stress.
- Your stress level is affected by different factors, including your support network, outlook, and ability to control your emotions.
- Many things may cause stress, such as school performance, financial conditions, and loss or grief.
- Stress can result from internal and/or external stressors.
- Problem-focused coping means taking action to solve the issue, and emotion-focused coping involves calming yourself down as well as separating yourself from the stressful situation.
- Active coping makes you want to resolve the problem right away, and avoidance coping

means that you prefer to procrastinate and ignore it.

- Coping mechanisms are divided into adaptive methods, which are helpful coping techniques, and maladaptive approaches, which are negative and harmful.
- To break maladaptive coping patterns, you can find a distraction, practice self-compassion, or meditate.
- Some healthy coping mechanisms to consider are exercising, exploring creativity, and establishing a support system.

In the next chapter, we'll discuss that nothing on social media is real and that you need to learn to accept and love yourself no matter what.

EMBRACE POSSIBILITIES

4

HERE'S THE TEA

Have you ever heard about Lizzo? Nowadays, she has become very famous, and her songs are being blasted everywhere we go. However, do you know that it took time for her to become who she is today? She's been making music for a long time, but she became known after releasing songs about self-love and self-acceptance, such as *Tempo, Truth Hurts, and Juice.* She's a plus-size woman who likes showing her body and curves to the world. Women with skinny bodies often dominate the music industry; when Lizzo showed up, it appealed to a lot of people because she celebrated herself, and it was refreshing to see a different type of body. Through her songs, she inspires other women to be proud of their bodies and spreads the message of body positivity and self-love. On her social media platforms, she shows and promotes that practicing self-love through self-acceptance and being true to herself helped her be the confident person everyone knows her to be. She doesn't care that others mock her for how she looks because she's comfortable with herself and her appearance.

IS SOCIAL MEDIA BAD FOR ME?

Vanessa was struggling with her self-image and self-worth. She felt she wasn't skinny enough like the girls she saw on social media. This made her very insecure, and she thought she wasn't pretty because her body was bigger. She was constantly self-conscious about her appearance and her fashion choices. As a teenager, she wanted to get validation from her followers on her Instagram. Then, she made a plan to reduce her weight as much as possible. The only way she knew how to do it was to skip meals. Other girls also talked about how they threw up their food after every meal, and Vanessa decided to try that as well. This made her suffer from an eating disorder. She indeed lost a lot of weight in a very short time, but her body also became frail.

However, she couldn't stop her bad eating habits because she started receiving compliments on social media and getting more followers on her account. She couldn't get enough attention, so she kept practicing unhealthy ways of dieting. Eventually, she had no energy to do anything in class because she got sleepy and hungry quickly. This made it hard for her to concentrate, which affected her grades negatively. Her relationship with her parents also suffered because she got angry at them whenever they told her to eat more. Vanessa must realize that nothing is real on social media and start living in the real world. She has to get help before she suffers from more health issues because an eating disorder can be very damaging to her body.

The Impact of Media on Your Mental Health

As humans, we need to connect and interact with each other to survive in this world. We'll feel better and happier when we have good relationships with others because they offer us a sense of belonging. It also helps us avoid mental health issues because our loved ones will be there for us when we need someone to listen to or advise us. If we don't have good relationships, it'll make us feel alone and isolated, which will negatively affect our mental well-being.

In this technological era, social media is used as a medium to stay connected with other people wherever they are. As a teenager, you must have been on different platforms like Instagram, TikTok, Facebook, or Snapchat to talk to your friends or meet new people. I know that social media has its advantages, but it's not the same as face-to-face interactions with people. Have you ever felt it's better to talk about something serious in-person rather than chatting? It's the same with connection because you can only connect fully with someone in real life. Social media was made to bring people closer together, but the truth is that those who spend too much time there will feel isolated from the real world.

Before we go further into the chapter, it's time for you to reassess how much of your time you spend on social media. If you find that you waste too much time there and start feeling lonely, frustrated, or sad, you need to take a step back and spend more time socializing with people in real life.

The Negative Aspects of Social Media

Various studies have discovered a substantial correlation between using social media excessively and a higher risk of depression, anxiety, and even self-harm (Robinson & Smith, 2023). There are many negative experiences that you may get from social media. Let's explore some of them:

- Poor body image: Influencers often flash their perfect lives on their social media accounts. I know that you can't help but envy them sometimes. Even if you know that not all of them are real, it's hard not to feel insecure when you compare them to your life. When we see girls with perfect skin, we wish we had that, even though we know they've edited their pictures. Social media creates unrealistic standards that most people can't meet, and it can cause a poor self-image.

- Cyberbullying: Since users of social media can remain anonymous and disguise their identities, it's simpler for them to bully one another online. Nowadays, social media platforms like Twitter and Instagram are used to spread gossip and lies with little or no consequences. About 10% of teenagers on social media reported being bullied, and countless others experienced rude and negative comments (Robinson & Smith, 2023).

- Fear of missing out (FOMO): Like an addiction, when you're scared of missing out on something, you'll lower your self-esteem and increase your worry. FOMO causes you to always keep looking at your phone for notifications, even if doing so puts your safety and that of other people at risk when walking along the road.

Causes of Unhealthy Social Media Use

Nowadays, the majority of us now use smartphones for browsing social media. I know that this helps us to connect with people online, but it also means that social media is always at our fingertips. This constant connection can lead to issues with our concentration and interfere with our sleep time because we keep wasting time on social media. Additionally, there are other factors that contribute to unhealthy social media use, such as the following:

- Avoiding Awkwardness: Have you ever turned to your phone when faced with an awkward situation? Using social media allows you to avoid having face-to-face interactions, which might reduce anxiety. For example, your mom asks you to meet her friends. Because you have nobody to talk to, you might feel awkward. By scrolling through social media, you don't have to face the awkwardness and may feel better even if no one talks to you.
- Concealing underlying issues: You might use social media to cover up issues like anxiety or

depression. Do you use social media more when you feel stressed out or lonely? If so, this might mean you're trying to block out negative emotions and boost your mood.

Warning Signs That Social Media Is Impacting Your Mental Health

You need to be aware of a few symptoms to determine whether social media is harming your mental health. Everybody is different, so only you can know if it negatively impacts you. Here are several warning signs to observe:

- Comparing yourself: If you see that you often compare yourself with influencers with perfect bodies and lives, it means that social media has affected you negatively. You may wish to be like them by following their lifestyles even though you can't afford them.
- Being distracted at school: Instead of focusing in class, you choose to open your social media to keep yourself updated. You care more about how many followers or likes you receive rather than getting good grades.
- Having no time for yourself: You spend every second of your life on social media and never

set aside time to think about your actions and behavior. When this happens, you can't grow and develop as a person.

Changing How You Use Social Media to Boost Your Mental Health

To boost your mental health, you need to try to limit your time on social media. One way to do this is by using a tracking app. This way, you can keep tabs on how much time you spend time each day on your phone and then decide how much you'd like to lower it. Another way is to prevent taking your electronics to your bedroom. When you're about to sleep, you should leave your phone or laptop in another room to charge so that it doesn't disturb your sleep. Lastly, you may put your phone on silent mode. It's tough to resist looking at your phone when you notice a notification. If your phone is silent, you can't hear anything, so you won't feel the need to constantly check your phone.

Additionally, you have to spend more time with people in real life. To make your mental health better, you need to talk and interact with others face-to-face without using social media. You can do this by making plans each week for your friends and family and leaving your phones at home whenever you hang out with them. You may also join extracurricular activities like art classes or sports clubs to interact with people with the same passions as you. Moreover, if you've neglected a friend because of social media, you should contact them again. You may ask them out for coffee or lunch together at the cafeteria.

Methods to Spend Less Time on Social Media

You can use a few techniques to cut down on your social media usage. Of course, you don't have to start big because starting with small steps is okay. During your classes, meals, or other activities, you can switch off your phone and focus on them. You can just silence the notifications if you don't want to turn it off. You may also make a timer for social media use. Perhaps you decide to only use your phone for 30 minutes at a time several times a day. When you're ready, you may delete unnecessary social media apps from your phone. You can still keep them on your laptop to talk to your friends, but when they're not on your phone, you can't access them that easily. Most importantly, you should find other hobbies or passions to distract yourself. Maybe you can start cooking new recipes, reading exciting novels, or writing short stories.

KEEPING IT REAL

What's good about social media? Even though it has some negative aspects, it also offers you some positive ones. One example of this is Lizzo: She's using her social media platform to promote inclusivity, body positivity, and self-love. She makes her social media accounts a safe space for insecure people so that they can accept and love themselves as well as be comfortable in their skin. Social media can also be useful for you as long as you use it responsibly and don't spend all of your time there. What other benefits do social media platforms offer?

- interacting and communicating with people across the world
- connecting with those with similar goals and passions
- looking for or providing emotional support for those in need
- discovering a way to express yourself and your imagination

How to Use Social Media to Your Advantage

It's possible to use social media to empower yourself. However, you have to go through a journey of self-love and self-acceptance first so that social media doesn't impact you negatively. You need to decide to love and accept yourself before anyone can do the same. Let's explore this topic more:

- Accepting yourself: Before you can love yourself, you need to practice acceptance. When you're used to talking down on yourself, it can be challenging at first. With social media, it's even harder because we're constantly exposed to unrealistic expectations and standards. Accepting yourself may simply involve embracing who you are as you are while still recognizing that you can always improve. You have your own journey, so there's no need to compare it to others.
- Being honest: Self-love is all about being honest. It means that you need to be honest with yourself that you deserve good things and express it to others. You don't have to always follow others' expectations because you'll never be happy. You can write down what you want and need in your journal and pursue them in real life. Be honest with yourself, and you'll find that you deserve more than you think.
- Following those who advocate for you: You might be tempted to follow influencers who always do good things, but it'll only give you

insecurities. Perhaps you can follow people with the same body type or life situations as you. These people might be more realistic with their lives and are not trying to sugarcoat anything. For instance, if your body type is like Lizzo, you can follow her on Instagram because she always promotes positivity on her account.

- Working out for yourself: Instead of getting fit to follow beauty standards, you should work out to feel better about yourself. Social media always tells us to exercise to achieve certain standards, but it's not good because not everyone will be able to accomplish them. What you need to do is work out to stay healthy rather than following aesthetic standards.

- Redefining beauty: Although it's impossible to always love each aspect of your body, you can change the way you think about it. Perhaps you think your thighs are too big. Why don't you reframe your thinking? Think of your thighs as things that are not ugly but rather as a feature that highlights your figure, so they're beautiful. You can move closer to loving yourself by changing the way you view your body and putting more emphasis on what it does for you than how it looks.

Let's take a look back at Vanessa's story. She was self-conscious of her appearance because she thought she wasn't skinny enough like the influencers on Instagram. To help her love and accept herself, Vanessa needs to follow people who advocate self-acceptance of physical flaws to spark positive thoughts about her looks.

BEING REAL IS THE NEW TREND

What do you think being authentic means? Some people think that being authentic means being trustworthy or honest; others may associate it more with being real and not fake (Lyons, 2021). Which one do you prefer? I think both are true because to be genuine, you need to become a trustworthy and honest person first.

What are the benefits of authenticity? Living an authentic life begins with self-reflection, where you learn about yourself and increase your awareness about your wants and needs. By doing this, you'll start becoming your true self in relationships, at home, and at school. By living authentically, you'll pay more attention to your values and worth. When this happens, you'll work to achieve your goals without having to follow others' expectations and standards. By being honest and genuine about yourself, no one will be able to influence you toward something negative.

Why Is it Difficult to be Authentic?

Being honest and genuine about yourself seems like a great idea that can make you happier and feel better, so why is it so hard to do? The first reason is that we don't want to stand out and be considered weird. When you stay true to yourself, you'll be different from others. As you know, there are various standards that you need to follow to fit in, so when you're unique, people will think that you're strange. It's easier to follow along so you don't become a misfit.

Another reason is that it might feel selfish to be authentic. It will eventually get tiresome to conform to what other people want you to be. For example, you're the class clown who becomes the life and soul of every situation. You know you don't enjoy it because all you want is a peaceful day, but you feel like you can't let people down if you stop making jokes. Here, you feel like you're not allowed to be quiet because then no one can smile or laugh.

How You Can Discover Your True Self

If you wish to live a more authentic life, there are ways to start accepting who you are. Loving yourself and living authentically will be a difficult journey, but the first step to self-love is self-acceptance. The following are some approaches to self-acceptance so that you can stay true to yourself:

- Recognize your strengths: One way to connect to your authenticity is to embrace your strengths. Pay close attention to activities you're good at but don't particularly love. For example, you're good at writing but don't enjoy doing it. You can find ways to make it more fun, like writing fanfiction about your favorite show or movie. Who knows, maybe you can even earn money with it.
- Identify your emotions: To be more authentic, you need to know how to recognize your emotions as they appear. When you feel angry, happy, or sad, you can try to understand why you're feeling them. This awareness will help you to find their sources and find ways to resolve them if they're negative.
- Learn to face your fears: You must have something that you fear, and you're trying your best to avoid it. However, if you want to live authentically, you need to face your fears with courage. Life can be an adventure, but if you only stay in your comfort zone, you'll never get the complete experience of life. For instance, if you're scared of public speaking, spend more

time talking to strangers so that you can get used to talking to an audience.

- Explore your values: By knowing your values, you'll have a direction to follow so that you don't get swayed easily by others. For example, suppose your value is to never cheat on an exam, even if everyone in your class decides to cheat. In that case, you won't follow them because you want to keep your integrity.

It can sometimes be difficult to accept after you've discovered your true self. Self-awareness and acceptance go a long way toward enhancing your mental health. Here are some tips on how to accept yourself:

- Forgive yourself: This helps you take responsibility for your actions because only then will it become possible for you to move on.
- Ignore your inner critic: There is always that voice inside telling us we are not good enough. Ignore it and take control of your mind because you are good enough.
- Move on from disappointments: It's normal to encounter disappointment; don't let them keep you stuck. Move on so that you can acknowledge and love your abilities.

SELF-LOVE EXERCISE

Practicing self-love doesn't have to be hard because there are many self-love exercises out there. Here, I'll let you know one of them to help you practice self-love better. The exercise is called "My Love Letter to Myself." This activity encourages self-love by writing love letters to yourself and highlighting your best qualities. This exercise will help you practice self-love and be kind to yourself, which will assist you in going through your life at school or home. How do you do this?

1. List some of the best qualities that you love the most.
2. Describe some instances in which these qualities have helped you in your daily life.
3. Write down different ways you can appreciate and honor these qualities.

For example, if you think that you're an honest person, you may say that being honest has helped you never cheat on your exams. To appreciate this quality, you can say, "I'll remind myself that I'm an honest person every day."

Key Takeaways

- Excessive social media use can have negative aspects on you, such as poor body image, cyberbullying, and FOMO.
- Why does unhealthy social media use happen? You might use it as a way to avoid awkwardness or conceal underlying issues like depression or stress.
- There are clear signs that social media is affecting your mental health, including comparing yourself to others, being distracted at school, and having no time for yourself.
- To improve your mental health, you need to limit your time on social media and spend more time with people in real life.
- Although it can have negative aspects, social media also has positive ones, like interacting and communicating with people all over the world.
- To use social media to your advantage, you have to love yourself first by accepting yourself, being honest, following those who advocate for you, working out for yourself, and redefining beauty.
- Being authentic is also essential to being genuine about who you are.
- Living an authentic life is hard because it makes you stand out, and it can feel like a selfish thing.

- To discover your authentic self, you need to recognize your strengths, identify your emotions, learn to face your fears, forgive yourself, and explore your values.

In Chapter 5, we'll discuss the importance of your mindset and how it can affect your self-confidence, as well as how to establish a growth mindset.

MAKE A DIFFERENCE WITH YOUR REVIEW

UNLOCK THE POWER OF GENEROSITY

"Giving is not just about making a donation. It is about making a difference."

— KATHY CALVIN

Helping others without expecting anything in return can make you feel amazing, and it can even help you live a happier, longer life! So, if we can make a difference together, let's give it a try.

To make this happen, I have a question for you...

Would you help someone you've never met, even if you never got credit for it?

Who is this person, you ask? They are just like you. Maybe they're younger or just starting out, eager to make a difference but unsure of where to begin.

Our mission is to make self-confidence and personal growth accessible to everyone. Everything I do stems from that mission. And the only way to reach everyone is with your help.

This is where you come in. Most people do, in fact, judge a book by its cover (and its reviews). So here's my ask on behalf of a struggling teen you've never met:

Please help that teen by leaving a review for this book.

Your gift costs no money and takes less than 60 seconds to complete, but it can change a fellow teen's life forever. Your review could help...

...one more teen believe in themselves. ...one more young person finds their courage. ...one more student face their fears. ...one more friend feel supported. ...one more dream come true.

To get that 'feel good' feeling and truly help someone, all you have to do is...and it takes less than 60 seconds...leave a review.

Simply scan the QR code to leave your review:

If you feel good about helping a faceless teen, you are my kind of person. Welcome to the club. You're one of us.

I'm that much more excited to help you build your confidence and reach your goals faster and easier than you can imagine. You'll love the tips and strategies I'm about to share in the coming chapters.

Thank you from the bottom of my heart. Now, back to our regularly scheduled program-ming.

- Your biggest fan, Michelle Ostan

PS - Fun fact: If you provide something of value to another person, it makes you more valuable to them. If you think this book will help another teen, please send this book their way.

5

WHAT'S A MINDSET?

Do you know the famous teen sitcom Hannah Montana? There's a song that I like from the show called *Nobody's Perfect*. The message of this song is that nobody in the world is perfect or flawless. As humans, it's normal to make mistakes sometimes. The song teaches us that no matter how perfect your plan is, mistakes may still happen because we can't predict the future. However, just because you can't always get things right the first time, it doesn't mean that you should give up. You need to recover and accept your mistakes so that you can get back up again. You can do better next time if you're willing to learn from your mistakes. Whether you decide to get up and try again or just give up because of your failure is all determined by your mindset.

WHY DOES MY MINDSET MATTER?

Jenny had been told by others that she wasn't smart because her family was poor. No one thought that she would do well in school because she didn't have access to tutoring like her other friends. They always said that she should've just gotten out of there to work and help support her family. As time passed, she took some classes and found that she did well in science classes like biology and chemistry. She enjoyed learning these subjects, but even though she did well, her grades were not perfect, and she wasn't on top of her class. Moreover, people had said that she would never become smart, so she decided not to try too hard. Since she refused to work hard, her grades became just average or even bad in other classes. This made her believe that all those people were right. Jenny saw herself negatively because of her family situation, which gave her low self-esteem and self-confidence. When she saw her friends with better financial situations, she would often get jealous because she couldn't get what they had. Here, it shows that Jenny has a fixed mindset because she thinks that she's not smart because of her poor family. Her mindset prevents her from succeeding at something even though she could put in the effort to do well in those science classes.

What Is a Mindset?

A mindset is a collection of views and beliefs that you have that influence what you do, think, feel, and experience (Davis, 2023). Because your actions and behavior are determined by your mindset, it'll affect your likelihood of success (or failure). This means that it's crucial to build particular mindsets so that you may achieve your dreams and live a happier life.

So, how do mindsets form? According to Carol S. Dweck (2007), your mindset was first formed during childhood from praising and labeling. In praising, she states that if your parents often use *personal praise* and label you as smart, it'll build a fixed mindset (Cherry, 2022d). Why? Because it tells you that you either have the skill or not, and you can't change it. However, if your parents use *process praise* and highlight the work you put in to accomplish something, you'll feel that your success is because of your effort (Cherry, 2022d). This will tell you that you have control over your successes through hard work. For instance, personal praise could sound like, "You got 100% on your exam! You're great at physics!" When using process praise, on the other hand, your parents might say, "I appreciate how diligently you studied for the physics test. Your hard work paid off!"

Labeling means assigning qualities to individuals according to stereotypes of their groups (Cherry, 2022d). For example, someone may say that girls are bad at sports because their bodies are weak. Or they might say that boys are not good in English class because they're too lazy to read. These negative stereotypes may also lead to a fixed mindset because they might believe them.

It's important to understand where your mindsets come from because they have a significant influence on how you'll handle obstacles in life. When your mindset is more positive, you'll be more willing to gain knowledge, put in the effort to achieve something and explore new activities. If you work hard, it'll be easier for you to achieve success at school. As you grow older, you'll face more obstacles. Your positive mindset is there to help you see challenges as a stepping stone rather than a reason to give up. However, if your mindset is negative, you'll choose to give up because you can never advance when faced with difficulties.

The Difference Between Fixed and Growth Mindsets

The two primary mindsets that we have are the growth and fixed mindsets. Those with a growth mindset tend to think that they can improve their skills by putting in the effort and working hard (Davis, 2023). When you have a growth mindset, you work more diligently and look for feedback when you feel like you're not progressing. You're eager to pick up new skills in order to achieve your objectives and enhance your quality of life. For instance, Nadya wants to become the school president, but she needs to be good at public speaking. Instead of giving up on her dream, Nadya decides to look for a coach to help her improve her public speaking skills.

However, those with a fixed mindset think that their skills and intelligence come naturally and can't be improved. With a fixed mindset, you can't achieve your dreams because you think that they're out of your abilities. If you have this mindset, it's time to wake up and change it into a growth mindset. For example, Daniel sees that there's a science competition, and he's interested in it. However, he decides not to join because he thinks that his knowledge is still lacking and other students are better than him.

How Your Mindset Affects Your Self-Esteem, Self-Confidence, and Performance

With a growth mindset, you can improve your self-esteem, self-confidence, and performance. It's easy to decide that you're not good at something when you fail at it. However, a growth mindset will help you to work harder, get better at it, and eventually become good. For example, if you're not good at public speaking, you'll work to make yourself more comfortable in front of an audience and talking to them. As a result, you'll feel proud of yourself for working hard and also improve your self-confidence. Because you work for your development, you increase your public speaking abilities, which will make your performance at school better.

A growth mindset also influences your happiness level. When you have a fixed mindset, you think you can never change it because that's how it's supposed to be. You refuse to take charge of your happiness, so you're stuck being depressed and stressed out. However, a growth mindset will make you accept your current situation and then find ways to feel more positive. You know that to get happiness, you need to work for it. For example, if you enjoy hiking, you'll ask your dad to do it with you so that you may feel better. When you're happier, it'll spread to other aspects of your life, which will increase your self-esteem, self-confidence, and performance.

EVERYBODY MAKES MISTAKE

You know that it's important to have a growth mindset so that you may improve your abilities. However, is a growth mindset the same as perfectionism? They're actually different. Let's explore more about perfectionism.

What is perfectionism in the first place? Those with perfectionism want everything they do to be perfect. They set incredibly high standards for themselves, even though it might seem impossible. You may think that being a perfectionist is a good motivation so that you can accomplish more, but this is not true. Perfectionism can lead to a negative outlook on life because you force yourself to be something you're not. Believe it or not, it may also result in various mental health issues like anxiety and depression (Heitz, 2017). When your mental health is affected negatively, you'll end up having no energy to do anything or reach success anymore. As a teenager, you're more prone to becoming a perfectionist because you want to stand out from your peers and reach your parents' expectations. You're often pressured to perform perfectly in your academics and extracurricular activities, including sports. This means that you have to do all these things at once, which can cause burnout.

What made you a perfectionist? What causes it? The likelihood of being a perfectionist can be influenced by a variety of things. Some of the factors are a fear of being judged or rejected by others, your parents setting unrealistic standards on you, low self-esteem, the desire for control, and societal expectations.

The Symptoms of Perfectionism

When you have perfectionism, you may struggle to forgive yourself if you make a mistake, and you become overly sensitive to criticism. Perfectionism can impact only one aspect or even more of your life. For instance, you become a perfectionist when it comes to only academics or academics and sports. The following are several more symptoms of perfectionism:

- spending too much time fixing or minimizing mistakes
- relying on achievements for your self-esteem
- talking negatively to yourself when there's a mistake
- being too ambitious
- having a hard time relaxing and expressing your thoughts and emotions
- becoming incredibly controlling in your relationships

The Effects of Perfectionism

Because perfectionism makes you put on some unrealistic and harsh expectations of yourself, there will be some negative effects that come with it. If you find that you're a perfectionist and some of these effects already affect you, perhaps it's time to get out of perfectionism.

The first negative effect of perfectionism is lower productivity. Perfectionists often procrastinate. Perfectionism makes you think that everything has to be perfect; when something is too difficult, you may choose to procrastinate getting it done to avoid making a less-than-perfect outcome. For example, you have a math assignment that you don't really understand. Instead of asking a classmate to help, you procrastinate on it because you refuse to admit that you can't do it perfectly.

The next one is tense relationships. Perfectionists will hold their loved ones to higher standards as well. By doing this, you'll strain the relationships because your friends and family may feel stressed about meeting your expectations. They might even choose to distance themselves from you to let go of the pressure. For instance, you expect your girlfriend to always put on makeup or fashionable clothes so that you both can look good in public. This will put pressure on her when she doesn't feel like dressing up.

Lastly, it makes you not present in the moment. Perfectionism makes you worry so much that you become oblivious to the things happening around you. Maybe you're worried about a small mistake you made on your exam, and you repeat it over and over again in your mind. This will then lead you to hate yourself and procrastinate because you're not willing to make another mistake.

In Jenny's story, it was shown that she had a fixed mindset while also having perfectionism. She thought that because of her poor family, she would never become as smart as other kids. Moreover, even though she did well in her science classes, her grades weren't perfect, so she decided to stop trying altogether. What Jenny needs to realize is that her family situation doesn't determine her intelligence because she can teach herself. There are books in the library available to everyone, so she should make use of them. Nothing can stop her from succeeding if she's willing to put in the effort and accept that she can't be perfect all the time.

How to Overcome Perfectionism

If you discover that perfectionism has been affecting your life severely, you should talk to an adult or counselor to help you to overcome it. However, if you think that it's still manageable, there are ways you can do it by yourself.

- **Set realistic goals and expectations**: By doing this, you'll stop aiming for impossible perfection. Instead, you may use the resources at your disposal to accomplish your goals.

- **Avoid procrastination**: Rather than focusing on the result, you should focus on the process. For instance, you can prevent getting overwhelmed by dividing your assignment into smaller steps so that you may gain a sense of achievement.
- **Pursue different passions**: You may find things that bring you happiness. Don't concentrate on mastering or perfecting one thing. For instance, you can discover new hobbies or skills like swimming, writing, or graphic design.

YOU'RE GETTING THERE!

Let's take a look back at Hannah Montana's song, *Nobody's Perfect*. The song teaches us to get back up again even after a failure because it happens sometimes. All you need to do is accept that you can make mistakes so that you can learn from them. When you try again after a failure, you'll build your resilience and adapt to challenging things even if they happen again in the future. In this section, we'll discuss more about resilience.

What is resilience? Before that, have you ever wondered how someone can stay calm, even when faced with obstacles, while others fall apart? This is what we call resilience. Those who have resilience can successfully move through the ups and downs of life and recover from hardships (Elizabeth, 2022). When faced with a challenging situation, there are two options: either you will allow your feelings to control you and get overwhelmed by them, or you'll encourage yourself and turn suffering into opportunities. An obstacle doesn't have to destroy your life, and this is why you need to learn how to be resilient.

Why is resilience so important? It's easy to feel over-whelmed when something doesn't go your way. With resilience, you'll turn your failure into success. Even if you've failed, you need to try again so that you can build resilience and finally achieve your goals. Being resilient also establishes your positive beliefs. Because you'll try again after a failure, you'll need to focus on your positive emotions for support. This means that resilience makes you think more positively even though you have to face a challenge. Most importantly, resilience helps you accept and embrace change. In this world, you need to keep changing to survive. You can't be resilient if you always stay in your comfort zone. What you need to do is accept the challenge and push yourself to create something better.

What Does Being Resilient Mean in Psychology?

Being resilient helps you do more than just bounce back from an obstacle. Psychology is aware that resilient people who experience major life events don't always bounce back easily; they frequently choose a different path (Sutton, 2019). Even though they aren't unaffected by what has occurred, the darkest times usually result in growth for resilient people. Here are some areas that resilience allows us to grow in (Neenan, 2018):

- **An updated or fresh self-image**: As you overcome different obstacles, you'll grow aware of your unknown skills.
- **Relationships with greater clarity and strength**: In times of difficulty, resilience helps you to distinguish between friends who are there to support you and the ones who have abandoned you. This means that you give priority to healthy relationships.
- **Adjusted priorities**: Because your perspective has been renewed, you may eliminate useless things and encourage meaningful goals, values, and ambitions.

This also means that you find a new purpose after

going through an obstacle, which will grow and strengthen your resilience.

How to Develop Resilience

Even if you're not born with good resilience, it's still possible to become more resilient with practice. To achieve this, here are some things you should integrate into your life:

- **Trust your abilities**: Your resilience can be built when you trust your capacity to handle life's hardships. This means that you need to believe in your abilities to face and deal with an obstacle. For instance, if you fail a test and you're given a chance to retake it, rather than giving up, you should trust that you can do it because you've decided to study more.
- **Stay positive**: Resilience heavily relies on optimism. This means that you should try to be optimistic even in the face of difficulties. I know that it can be tough, but it's still possible to be hopeful even on the darkest day. Believe that the future is going to be better and that these obstacles are only temporary.
- **Take care of yourself**: When faced with hardships, it's easy to put off taking care of your

personal needs. Maybe you refuse to eat, skip going to the gym, or lock yourself in your room. However, you should take care of yourself even while you're struggling because it may make you feel better and give you the strength to face your challenges. For example, you can do things that you enjoy, like taking a hot bath, strolling around the park, or spending time with your friends.

- **Set goals**: An obstacle can be frightening and scary. They can appear impossible to solve. With resilience, you can approach these problems rationally and establish practical goals to address the issue. When you find yourself feeling overwhelmed, you should take a step back to evaluate it. Once your mind is in the right place, you may create a list of potential solutions and divide them into achievable steps.

GROWTH MINDSET EXERCISE

The exercise for a growth mindset is assessing your rejections. Everyone has been rejected for something at some point. To guarantee that upcoming situations are less disastrous, it can be beneficial to reflect on your rejections and answer some questions about growth.

Consider an instance where you experienced rejection. Maybe you weren't chosen for the volleyball team, were rejected by your crush, or didn't get an offer from a part-time job.

Questions	Answers
What can you learn from these instances?	
Has the experience given you a better understanding of who you are and what you want and don't want from life?	
What benefits can you get from being rejected in the future?	
Are you willing to forgive the person who rejected you and allow the resentment to leave your mind?	

KEY TAKEAWAYS

- Your mindset is important because it impacts your behavior, actions, and attitude in life.
- Your mindset is formed during childhood because of the impact of praise and labeling.
- It's essential because it can help you overcome

obstacles and plays a big role in your success (or failure).

- A fixed mindset is when you believe that you're born with your abilities and you can't change them. Meanwhile, a growth mindset makes you think that your skills can be improved through hard work.
- Perfectionism happens when you set unrealistic standards for yourself, which puts you under a lot of pressure.
- Being a perfectionist has some negative effects, such as having low productivity, creating tense relationships, and taking your focus away from the present.
- To overcome perfectionism, you should set realistic expectations for yourself and others, avoid procrastination, and pursue different passions.
- You also need to learn how to be resilient because it can help you bounce back after a challenge.
- In psychology, it's explained that being resilient offers you a new path and renewed life purpose.
- To build resilience, you have to trust your abilities, stay positive, practice self-care, and set goals.

Chapter 6 discusses the power of friendship and belonging and how you can still be yourself with the right group of friends. You'll also learn peer pressure and peer influence so that you may establish boundaries by discovering your goals and values.

SEEK TO TRANSFORM

WHAT'S THE VIBE?

The movie *Mean Girls* tells the story of a new student named Cady Heron. She was always homeschooled and never socialized with kids her age because her parents worked in the African jungle. When she left Africa, she needed to learn how to interact with teenagers in high school, which she found harder than her life in the jungle. Struggling to find her place and identity, she found herself with a group of girls called the Plastics, with Regina as their leader. In this group, she found out about the *Burn Book*, where the girls would write down nasty secrets and gossip about every other girl in their class and the teachers. At first, Cady didn't want to write anything, but she was pressured by the others and finally decided to join in. In the end, the book was used by Regina to take revenge on Cady, and she was blamed for it. From this story, you can see that it's hard to say no to peer pressure, especially when it means either fitting in or not. However, it didn't end up well for Cady because she had to face the consequences of following the girls' actions in the *Burn Book.*

FIGHTING THE PRESSURE

Kendall had always been a good student because she got excellent grades and only hung out with the "nerds" at school. Her life changed when she started dating one of the popular boys, Bryce. Her boyfriend didn't like her current friends because they weren't fun and convinced Kendall to start hanging out with the popular girls. Bryce started introducing her to some girls who were known to bully the nerds, even her, at some point. Because of the pressure, Kendall decided to listen to him and left her friends to gain popularity. To fit in the group, she had to follow what they did, like bullying others, partying, and skipping class. She let go of herself and started losing direction. Her old friends refused to talk to her, and her grades began dropping. She also started losing her identity because she became like the popular girls. She had abandoned her old hobbies like reading and writing and only cared about shopping for expensive clothes and makeup products.

Before she fails all of her classes and loses her friends, Kendall needs to change her priorities and seek help.

What Is Peer Pressure?

Peer pressure happens when people from your group of friends persuade or influence you to do certain things (Morin, 2022). As a teenager, you're more prone to peer pressure because you want to fit in with your friends. You may think that peer pressure is a negative influence to do bad things, but sometimes, it can also be positive. For instance, your smart friend in class influences you to study together to pass an exam or get into a competition. This is why you need to be careful in choosing the right group of friends to hang out with.

How can peer pressure affect you? Certain types of peer pressure may be simpler to recognize than others because they can be small or big. To handle peer pressure better, you need to identify how it affects you first. The following are some indications that you may be exposed to peer pressure:

- feeling like you're a misfit
- experimenting with new makeup or clothes trends in order to fit in
- comparing yourself to other kids
- being extremely self-conscious
- avoiding social interactions

Types of Peer Pressure

Because you wish to fit in with the crowd, you're willing to follow what other teenagers are doing so that you don't get made fun of or cast out. Before you can deal with it, you must learn the types of peer pressure and understand what's good and bad for you. Here are several types of peer pressure to help you make better and healthier choices in your teenage years:

- **Positive**: This refers to the positive encouragement and push friends give you to help you improve. Examples of this are asking your friends to study more diligently to get good grades or convincing others to volunteer at a homeless shelter.
- **Negative**: This involves pressure to commit something risky or harmful for yourself and other people. For instance, you influence a classmate to engage in bullying or force someone to use drugs.
- **Spoken**: This refers to the pressure that happens when someone asks you to do something. For example, your group of friends is pushing and asking you to smoke a cigarette.
- **Unspoken**: This happens when you follow along with what others are doing even when they don't ask you to. Maybe you follow your

friends' fashion choices or join clubs that others like.

- **Direct**: This peer pressure typically focuses on behaviours because you're put in the spotlight and forced to make a decision right away. It can be spoken as well as unspoken (Saxena & Sookdeo, 2020). Perhaps your friend hands you a glass of alcohol at a party, and you feel like you need to drink it because others are watching.
- **Indirect**: Even though this type is less obvious and more subtle, it still has a significant impact on you as a teenager (Saxena & Sookdeo, 2020). For instance, you hear your friends gossiping about a girl, and you join in with them.

The Effects of Peer Pressure

As you grow up, your friends will have a stronger influence on you. They can impact your passions, fashion style, and the music you listen to. It would be best if you filtered which influences are good and which are bad in order to avoid the bad ones. Moreover, peer pressure can affect you in both negative and positive ways.

Here are some advantages that you may gain from peer pressure:

- **Motivation**: Your friends may motivate you to try new activities that you've never thought of before, such as joining a science competition or auditioning for a play.
- **A support system**: Your closest friends can offer you support and give you solutions to your problems so that you may feel more confident facing challenges.
- **Good examples**: Positive friends will discourage you from having negative habits like spreading rumors and promote positive ones like exercising more.

Peer pressure also has some drawbacks:

- **Isolation from friends and family**: Toxic peer pressure tends to make you feel terrible about yourself, and this will create distance between you and your loved ones.
- **Academic distractions**: When you engage in harmful behaviors like drinking alcohol or doing drugs, you'll abandon your school priorities.

- **Unexpected behavioral shifts**: Trying to fit in with societal standards may cause you to start acting differently and lose your identity to follow others.

How to Handle Peer Pressure

It's essential to understand how to handle and say no to peer pressure. When you find yourself taking a bad turn and starting to follow negative peer pressure, you should stop it before you get in too deep. To help yourself say no to peer pressure, the following techniques can be beneficial.

The first method is preparing in advance. You can consider some things that you may feel pressured to do and prepare how you'll handle them. For instance, if you feel uncomfortable when someone asks you to drink because you're underage, you should leave the party. Perhaps you can contact trusted people like your parents or friends when you're in this situation.

Additionally, you may establish relationships with the right friends. Toxic friends will often bully you to do dangerous things like them. Even though you don't want to do them, you might feel pressured by the need to be accepted. This is why it's crucial to find good friends who can encourage you to do positive things like studying more or staying away from alcohol.

The final way is to talk to an adult. Suppose you're experiencing peer pressure that is difficult to control or stay away from. In that case, you should seek help from a trusted person like a teacher or parent. Let them know about your struggles, and they'll give you advice on how to get away from them. They may also help you prepare ahead of time before you face peer pressure.

BACKING UP A BIT

In Cady's story, you may see that she was willing to follow what the Plastics were doing because she wanted to fit in. It's a common phenomenon among teenagers because you need to feel like you belong to feel good about yourself. When you're insecure among others, you'll not feel positive about yourself. Moreover, if you don't have many friends, you might also feel isolated and have a bad self-image. As a teenager, a sense of belonging is essential for your development. You generally derive most of your identity from your friends since they frequently share your passions and world-views. When your friend group is positive, they'll help you feel like you belong while supporting your mental and emotional health development.

You'll establish better relationships and make healthy decisions when you feel comfortable in your friend group. You'll feel empowered during your teenage years because of the respect and confidence a sense of belonging fosters. These friends also help you go after your goals because you want each other to succeed. However, belonging does not mean sacrificing your own identity, and that's when boundaries come in.

Why Are Boundaries Important?

Boundaries are hypothetical lines separating you from people, which divide your personal space, desires, and obligations from those of others (Martin, 2018). They're made for your comfort around others and also define what is and is not acceptable in how people treat you. Others might want to use you if you don't set boundaries. When someone crosses your boundary, you must speak up and explain that it's wrong. Boundaries are useless if you don't enforce them with consequences.

Why is it important to set boundaries? Everyone has personal boundaries that help them better navigate life and social interactions. The fact is that everybody has their own unique boundaries that they need to communicate so that others can understand. Nobody will know your boundaries if you refuse to express them. The fundamental purpose of setting boundaries is to communicate your needs so that you may have healthy relationships with others. However, it's not always that simple because not everybody will get why you're setting boundaries in the first place. Setting boundaries frequently requires bravery and power, though you may relax once your boundaries have been established because you've told others what you need. You also have the right to stay away from those who refuse to follow your boundaries even after you try to enforce them (Campbell, 2023).

What Boundaries Do You Have to Set?

To know what boundaries to set, you have to observe which aspects of life you're having issues with. Do you frequently feel worn out at school? Do you feel uneasy with a classmate? Does your dad or mom often make you feel upset at home? All of these issues are indicators that you haven't set boundaries. The following are several typical types of boundaries to set:

- **Time**: Time boundaries help you safeguard the use of your time. They prevent you from getting burned out, letting others waste your precious hours, and being forced to do something (Martin, 2020). For instance, your evenings are set aside to spend with your parents, and you'll reply to your friends' texts about school or assignments in the morning.
- **Physical**: These boundaries help you protect your body and space. You have the right to

privacy and not be touched when you don't want to be (Martin, 2020). You may communicate the degree of physical contact that is okay for you and how others may act in your personal space. For example, if a stranger sits too close to you on the bus, you can move aside or choose to stand up.

- **Mental**: They protect what you think and feel because you have the right not to be judged. Sometimes, you can be selfish about your emotions to protect yourself without having to care what people feel and think. Perhaps when your friend wants to talk about sensitive topics like the death of a loved one, you may tell them that you're uncomfortable because you've just lost your grandpa too.
- **Material and financial**: They protect your belongings so that others don't take them without asking. For instance, you may ask your roommate not to take your food in the fridge without asking for permission. You also have the right to use your money as you see fit.

How to Establish Boundaries

Do you want to start setting boundaries with the people around you? Let's say you wish to establish them with your family or friends, but you're concerned about how it might affect your relationships. Perhaps you're worried that you may offend them or that they won't listen to you when you establish the boundaries. Let's explore some tips to establish boundaries:

- **Communicate clearly**: When you want to establish boundaries with others, you must communicate them openly and not just think about them in your mind. You might think that others should know how to behave around you even when you don't tell them anything, but this is simply impractical. Nobody will understand your boundaries if you haven't set the line. For example, you might ask your friend or family member to talk face-to-face in a quiet place. Before talking, breathe deeply, summon your courage, and then politely and directly express your boundaries.
- **Be mindful of how you speak**: Maybe you're scared about upsetting your friend or family member when setting boundaries. This is why you must be careful with the words you choose so that it doesn't sound like a personal attack to them. Instead of saying, "You always come into my room without my permission, and you shouldn't do that anymore," you might try saying, "I feel uncomfortable when you enter

my room without telling me. I understand we're best friends, but I'd appreciate your asking for my permission next time." There are ways to establish boundaries that don't seem aggressive.

- **Plan beforehand**: You should prepare what you'll say to the other person before meeting them. Perhaps you can write down your words and speak out loud in front of the mirror. This way, you can assess your words and change the ones that are not suitable. This will also prepare you to be more confident to talk if you get nervous easily.

How Well-Established Boundaries Help You Keep Your Identity and Handle Peer Pressure

Boundaries help you put yourself first. They make you more aware of yourself and your relationships. That's why they're crucial for self-care and prioritizing yourself. Suppose you experience feelings of unhappiness, resentment, and identity loss. In that case, it's time to reassess your boundaries and observe if they're healthy or unhealthy. Healthy boundaries assist you in keeping your identity because you express your needs without having to win over others or please them. This means that when there's peer pressure in your friend group, you can say no to it because your boundaries act as a limit that others shouldn't cross without your permission. It's also important to find the right group of friends that can help you reach your personal goals or even find the direction in which you want to go.

REDEFINING GOALS

In Kendall's story, you may see how she lost herself after getting into a relationship with the popular boy, Bryce. She used to be a good student who got good grades and spent her time with the smart kids, but she changed because of her boyfriend's pressure. To get back in the right direction, Kendall needs to check herself and set the right goals for her future. This way, she may start to prioritize what truly matters to her and have the wisdom to say no to things that don't align with her goals. Let's talk more about goal setting in this section.

The Importance of Goal Setting

Goal setting refers to the process of determining the objectives you want to accomplish and involves identifying what must be done and coming up with a plan for carrying it out (Ho, 2023). But why is it so crucial to establish goals? The direction and purpose that goals offer are what make them valuable. You give yourself a vision and target to work on when you establish a goal. This will make your life more organized and purposeful by looking forward to the outcome. Goal setting also fosters a lot of positive things. You'll gain more motivation and encouragement because you know you want to work toward achieving your goals to get a better future. Your goals will guide you to make the changes you want. Additionally, they can be relied on to develop stronger relationships, boost your mental health, and improve your performance at school. When you have goals, you'll concentrate your attention on the things that matter. They enable you to envision the kind of life you want to live. When you're working toward a goal, you frequently put more time and effort into it and come up with clever ways to get there.

Types of Goals

As you grow up, there will be so many goals that you can set in your life. Goals can be set for the long term or short term; it all depends on what you wish to achieve. Here are some common goals that you can establish:

- **Education**: Passing a math exam, graduating from high school, or learning a new subject.
- **Health**: Working out to lose weight, competing in a race, taking up a new sport, or drinking less sugary drinks.

- **Family and relationship**: Getting closer to your crush, spending more time with your parents, or making new friends.
- **Financial**: Saving money to buy a PlayStation 5 or making a budget plan to reduce your spending.
- **Creativity**: Learning to play the guitar, trying out new cooking recipes, or writing poems to post on a blog.

The Difference Between Goals and Values

Many people think that goals and values are the same, but they're not. They're different because goals typically have clear, measurable targets that can be checked off as accomplished, while values are what you think matters more in your life and are typically continuous because they have no result or end (*Goal Setting*, 2021). When your goals are rooted in your values, they have a higher chance of being achieved. For instance, if maintaining connections with your loved ones is a priority, your goals can be spending more quality time with your girlfriend or boyfriend and setting aside your weekends to hang out with your family members.

The Impact of Goal Setting on Your Mental Health, Self-Confidence, and Self-Identity

Goal setting is excellent for your mental health because it can make you happier. When you succeed in accomplishing your goals, you'll feel proud of your effort and experience an increase in self-esteem. You'll feel like your struggles in life are getting easier because each goal you achieve boosts your happiness. Goal setting also offers you worthwhile learning opportunities that will enhance your quality of life. From your goals, you'll learn valuable things like resilience, independence, and compassion. Other advantages of goal setting are providing you with a purpose and direction and giving you a sense of responsibility. When all of these benefits are combined, they'll help you improve your mental health and control your emotions better.

Goal setting not only has an impact on your mental health, but it also influences your self-confidence and self-identity. When you accomplish a goal, you'll also feel more confident about your abilities. This is because you do your best to achieve a goal, and that's what makes it possible. On the way to achieving your goals, you'll be tested by stress and doubt. Once you reach the end goal, you know it's because of your determination and effort. You'll also learn more about yourself in the course of it all. You'll understand the aspects that you're good or bad at. This means that you find your self-identity so that you may work to improve your weaknesses and take advantage of your strengths.

To achieve better mental health, self-confidence, and self-identity, your goals don't have to be big or grand. Small goals work just as well. What matters is that you put enough time and energy into achieving the goals in order to feel good about yourself.

How to Set Attainable Goals

Choosing your goals is very simple, but coming up with a strategy to achieve them can be difficult and overwhelming. In this section, I'll let you know the secret to achieving what you want through SMART goals. This method allows you to include detailed actions you must do to reach your goals. SMART is an acronym for specific, measurable, achievable, relevant, and time-based (Herrity, 2023). Let's explore each of these points:

- **Specific**: You must create a specific goal first. You may ask some of these questions: What do I hope to achieve? Will reaching this objective have a significant effect on my life? What steps do I have to plan? For instance, your goal could be to pass the biology class.
- **Measurable**: The goal can be measured since this will make it easier to track, and you

may see the changes step by step. For example, the biology class can be passed if you've understood the 12 chapters of the workbook.

- **Achievable**: You have to make sure that you have the resources to achieve the goal. This means that you need to make sure you have the workbook and then set aside time to study every chapter in it.
- **Relevant**: The goal should also be relevant. You need to pass the biology class because it'll help you graduate high school.
- **Time-based**: You need to set a specific deadline for your goal, and it needs to be realistic too. For example, you give yourself three months to study and understand every chapter in the biology book.

KEY TAKEAWAYS

- Peer pressure occurs when someone influences you to do something because you want to fit in with them.
- Some indications that show you're being peer pressured are feeling like a misfit, experimenting with new trends to fit in, comparing yourself to others, etc.

- Some types of peer pressure are negative, positive, spoken, unspoken, direct, and indirect.
- Peer pressure has some benefits, like serving as motivation, growing your support system, and setting good examples. However, it also has drawbacks, such as isolation from friends and family, academic distractions, and unexpected behavioural shifts.
- To say no to peer pressure, you should prepare ahead, establish relationships with the right friends, and talk to an adult.
- Boundaries are made for your comfort so that people don't take advantage of you and to help you navigate life and social interactions better.
- Some types of boundaries you can set are time, physical, mental, and financial and material.
- To establish boundaries, you have to communicate them clearly, be mindful of how you speak, and plan beforehand.
- You set boundaries to prioritize yourself so that you can keep your identity and handle peer pressure.
- Goal setting is crucial because it provides you with direction and concentration.
- Some common areas for the goals you may set are education, health, family and relationships, finances, and creativity.

- Goal setting impacts your mental health, self-confidence, and self-identity because it makes you happier, feel proud of yourself, and get to know who you are on a deeper level.
- You establish attainable goals through the SMART method by setting specific, measurable, achievable, relevant, and time-based goals.

The next chapter explores the importance of emotions and how you can manage them and improve your communication skills to deepen your relationship with others.

7

THEY JUST DON'T UNDERSTAND ME

ever Have I Ever is a TV show that tells the story of Devi Vishwakumar. After her father's death, she suffered psychological trauma that left her unable to move her legs for a few months. After a disastrous first year in high school, she wished to improve her status socially, but other people and her emotions made it difficult for her. As she went through grief and school life, Devi struggled to connect with her mother, Nalini. The show showed how they didn't know how to communicate with each other, which led to many misunderstandings. They had no idea how to process their grief and emotions, and it strained their relationship. What they needed to do was communicate and express their needs and feelings to strengthen their connection.

WHAT'S HAPPENING TO ME?

June had been struggling with his sexuality. He felt that he was more attracted to boys than girls and thought that there was something wrong with him. June couldn't accept who he was. He also didn't know how to communicate this with his parents because he was scared of how they might react. He often felt overwhelmed and lashed out at his family and argued with them. Many people told him that he was in control of his emotions, but he didn't feel that way. He tried talking to his friends and a counsellor at school, but nothing worked. He ended up treating his family poorly because he got irritated easily even though he hadn't expressed his feelings. When they tried to talk to him, he avoided their questions. This caused their relationship to strain and put so much stress on him. His performance at school also suffered because he got distracted by thinking about his sexuality and relationship with his family all the time. I think that June needs to be open and communicate more with his parents. Even if he doesn't want his parents to know about his sexuality, he should regulate his emotions better.

Why Do Teens Experience Mood Swings?

As a teenager, I'm sure that you've experienced the ups and downs of moods. Perhaps you feel so excited and happy one day but sad and empty the next. Don't worry; this is normal because you're experiencing a lot of changes socially, emotionally, and physically. Because of all these changes, you'll be more susceptible to mood swings. Let's explore more about each of these factors.

Socially, you'll have to form new connections and relationships with your friends. These relationships will not always go smoothly because there may be drama involved, and they'll influence your emotional state. As you form new relationships, you separate yourself from your parents. Being independent will create a sense of responsibility that may add stress and pressure to your life.

Emotionally, you'll want others to accept you. You want to avoid becoming a misfit, so you try your best to follow along. But you may feel more agitated and anxious as a result. You'll worry too much about giving good impressions to everyone around you.

Physically, you go through puberty in your teenage years. Your body will change, and your hormones will fluctuate more often. When this happens, your mood will have its ups and downs. Your brain also matures, which will help you regulate and take control of your emotions better (Why Teens Have Mood Swings: Exploring Emotional Vulnerability, 2023).

As you become aware of your emotions because of these changes, it's normal to experience mood swings because you're on a journey of self-discovery. These changes may also cause you stress because you're put under pressure to create new relationships, deal with new emotions, and face physical transformations. This is why it's essential to recognize your emotions and process them first before you respond.

MANAGING EMOTIONS

Before you can take control of your emotions, you must first understand where they originate from. So, where do emotions come from? A network of interlinked parts of the brain called the limbic system is responsible for our emotions (Cherry, 2023). Every emotion has a distinct location in the brain; for instance, the amygdala (one part of the limbic system) is involved in processing emotions like fear (Zimmerman, 2023). In conclusion, your emotions are made by your brain.

How Do Emotions Impact You, and Why Are They So Important?

Emotions can impact you physically. When you experience an emotion, you may have felt that your body also reacts to it. For example, your cheeks turn red when you feel shy, or your chest tightens, and your heart rate increases when you're scared or anxious (Lindsey, 2023). Moreover, when you suppress your emotions, it'll impact how you behave and carry yourself. When you're feeling low or insecure, you'll tend to walk with your head down and slump your shoulder. If you're happy, you'll also find your face is filled with smiles or laughs, and your heart rate may also increase.

But why are emotions so important? Many benefits can be gained from your emotions. The following are some of them:

- **They motivate you**: Let's say that you have an upcoming presentation. Because you want to do well, you'll feel various emotions like nervousness, excitement, and anxiety. These emotions will motivate you to practice more. You're more likely to take action and improve yourself positively to achieve a good grade on the presentation.
- **They help you avoid danger**: Perhaps you're walking alone at night. You then see a stranger walking behind you, and it makes you feel scared and anxious. These emotions help your body to prepare to act by running away or walking faster to get away from the stranger.
- **They help people understand you**: When you talk to someone, it's essential to offer clues to

show what you feel. For instance, when you feel happy about what your friend is talking about, you'll show them through your facial expressions, like smiling.

How to Handle Your Emotions

In June's story, you may see how he didn't know how to communicate his sexuality to his parents. He thought that there was something wrong with him and was scared of his family's reaction. To handle his emotions better, June needs to find ways to handle his emotions to avoid lashing out at his parents and worsening his relationship with them. Here are some ways to deal with your emotions better:

- **Recognize them**: To take control of your emotions, you should check in with yourself and identify what you're feeling. Let's say you have a boyfriend. You tried to meet him at school and plan a date night, but he said that he was too busy. The following week, you tried again, but he kept avoiding you. This made you very sad and upset, and you decided to throw away your phone or become rude to him. This is when you should take a step back and reframe your thoughts. You need to ask yourself these questions: What am I feeling?

What causes me to feel these emotions? What do I want to do in response to them? Is there a more effective method of handling them? By answering these questions, you'll find that destroying your phone or being rude is not the answer. You'll also avoid damaging the relationship even further.

- **Accept them**: When you try to regulate your emotions better, you may want to downplay them to yourself. For instance, you want to cry and scream because you didn't get an offer from your dream university. You might think that it's better to say, "I should just relax because it's not a big deal." However, this statement invalidates your emotions even though you know this is important to you. This is why you must accept your emotions and find comfort with them. You can avoid extreme, destructive reactions by processing strong emotions more deeply and increasing your comfort level with them (Raypole, 2023). Perhaps you may say, "I'm so sad about getting rejected from that university, but I can try again next year and study more."

- **Give yourself some space**: When you're feeling intense and strong emotions, it can help to separate yourself from them to ensure that you can respond to them appropriately. Maybe you decide to leave an uncomfortable situation or distract your mind to help you put distance between yourself and what's causing the intense emotions. Once your mind is calm, you can then get back to the emotions to deal with them. Some distractions you may consider are taking a walk, talking to your best friend, watching YouTube videos, etc.

Asking for Help From a Trusted Adult

I know that it's important to try to manage our own emotions. However, there will be times when you need help to handle them. When things get too overwhelming, you must get help from a trusted adult like a parent or teacher. Here are some signs to watch out for so that you know when to ask for help:

- You have trouble falling asleep at night or wake up often during your sleep.
- Your energy level drops, and you start to lose hope as well as get easily discouraged.
- You use alcohol or drugs to distract yourself.
- You're getting into fights with your friends.

TELLING THEM HOW YOU REALLY FEEL

At the end of Devi and Nalini's story, they finally find common ground. They begin understanding each other because they start communicating their needs and emotions. They open their minds so that they can listen to one another to better their relationship as mother and daughter. Devi wasn't able to grieve properly because Nalini also didn't know how to process it. Nalini was supposed to lead Devi so that they could be close to each other and process her dad's death together. Parents should support and motivate their children to get out of a bad situation and build their self-confidence to face challenges. A parent needs to know how to communicate and express what's important for their children's development.

The Importance of Having a Support System

I know that sometimes you might want to do things alone. However, if you always do so, it may leave you feeling isolated and lonely. This is why it's crucial to nurture your relationships with others and establish a strong support system. If you take a look back, you'll realize that you leaned on your friends and family for various things. Asking for help doesn't make you weak but gives you strength. When you have people to depend on, you'll become more confident in facing life's obstacles. You don't have to solve problems by yourself because they'll offer you solutions. For instance, you're being bullied at school. Your parents are your support system, and you decide to tell them. They may help you get a counselling session and address the issue with your principal. A strong support system also helps create better self-awareness. Those in your support system may give you honest and genuine feedback for your own good. They make you aware of your mistakes and flaws so that you can better yourself. Maybe you don't realize that you're rude to your servers at restaurants. Your friend may point this out and let you know that this behavior is wrong.

PRACTICAL TIPS TO IMPROVE COMMUNICATION SKILLS

Communication skills are essential for expressing your feelings. When you don't know how to communicate well, you'll have a hard time making others understand your perspective. Communication skills also help you decrease misunderstandings because you're willing to listen too. You understand the message being said and process it before you form a response. Let's explore some practical tips to develop your communication skills:

- **Listen more**: When you communicate with someone, it's essential to listen to them. Nobody will like talking to you if you're not willing to focus on what they have to say. To prevent misunderstandings, you may also ask for clarification on things you don't understand. For instance, when talking to your mom on the phone, you should refrain from texting at the same time because you should give her your full attention.

- **Know your audience**: The way you speak relies on who the other person is. It's alright to talk with informal language when talking to a friend, but you shouldn't do it when speaking to a teacher or boss. For example, when talking to your teacher, try not to use too much slang that they might not understand.

- **Watch your body language**: When interacting with someone, you need to use open body language to make them feel welcome and comfortable. You shouldn't cross your arms because that communicates that you're not willing to listen, and you should try to keep proper eye contact to demonstrate that you're paying attention to the conversation. In a video call, you should try looking directly into the camera instead of your phone.

- **Smile more**: People will be comfortable when talking to you when you show that you're positive and give them a warm smile. I know that it sounds simple, but you'll see that it may have a significant influence on your conversation. For instance, before speaking to someone, you need to smile and express your excitement about talking to them.

KEY TAKEAWAYS

- Teens typically experience mood swings because they experience many changes in their social life, emotional state, and physical appearance.
- Emotions have an impact on your body, such as your cheeks turning red when you feel shy or embarrassed.
- Your emotions are important because they motivate you, help you avoid danger, and help people understand you.
- To handle your emotions better, you must try to recognize them, accept them, and give yourself some space.
- However, when you can't deal with your emotions alone, you should seek help from a trusted adult.

- Some advantages of having a support system are improved self-confidence, emotional support, and better self-awareness.
- You can develop your communication skills by listening more, knowing your audience, watching your body language, and smiling more.

In Chapter 8, we'll discuss the importance of stepping outside of your comfort zone and how this can ultimately challenge you and develop your self-confidence.

8

A CONFIDENCE BOOSTER

The story of Troy Bolton and Gabriella Montez, who find their singing potential, is depicted in the film *High School Musical*. Troy was a basketball athlete, and Gabriella was a math whiz. They met at a winter break party and were asked to sing a duet for karaoke. At that party, they found out that their voices were good and they might have a talent for singing. After that, they thought of auditioning for the school musical. However, they were both still hesitant because they needed to feel more confident about their singing skills. When Gabriella finally found the courage to go on stage, the drama teacher announced that the audition was over. Troy also stepped forward to help Gabriella, but the teacher left the room. Then, they discovered that the musical composer dropped the music sheet and decided to sing the song together. The teacher overheard their performance and was impressed. When the teacher gave them another chance to audition for the roles, they both tried to pursue their passion for singing in secret and using their friends' help to prepare for it.

THE ONLY WAY TO KNOW IS TO TRY

Sarah was an aspiring writer who enjoyed writing fantasy novels on *Wattpad*. She got many positive comments on her books, and her readers enjoyed reading them. Some of them even encouraged her to go to a publisher so that she could profit from her writing. However, Sarah hesitated because she thought her work wasn't good enough to be published. But she still listened to her readers' suggestions and decided to talk to her parents about it. She asked her parents to read her books so that they could give her feedback. After reading the books, her parents were impressed and agreed with the readers' suggestions. They also told her that they'd help her find a suitable publishing house. Sarah decided to go out of her comfort zone and sent a script of her most popular book to a publisher. After several months, they informed her that they were going to publish her book.

Why Is It So Hard to Leave My Comfort Zone?

A comfort zone is a state that makes you feel secure (Page, 2020). In this state, you feel confident about your situation because you can predict what's going to happen. It also makes you feel in control since you know what to expect.

Why is fear part of leaving your comfort zone? Well, it's because things are uncertain outside, and as humans, our minds tell us to stay as comfortable as possible. You also fear the unknown. You'll have many questions in your mind, such as: *Can I become successful? Will I survive outside of my comfort zone? What if I fail?* Moreover, you'll also face a lot of pressure that makes you scared. Pressure causes stress, so it's normal to fear leaving your comfort zone. Fear is always part of the process, and the only way to overcome it is by facing it.

What Are the Advantages of Leaving Your Comfort Zone?

I understand that you might not want to leave your comfort zone because it's chaotic out there, but stepping out is essential for your development. Here are several benefits you'll gain by leaving your comfort zone:

- **It makes you stronger**: I know that it can be scary when you step out of your comfort zone, and you may feel insecure at times. It's normal to feel uncertain about your life when you're trying to navigate situations outside of your comfort zone. You might even fail on your journey, but you should face your failure with a positive mentality. You develop the most when you can get back up after a failure. This means that you'll also grow stronger as you move forward.

- **It helps you meet new people and gain positive experiences**: Leaving your comfort zone means that you'll try new activities and hobbies. In these situations, you may make new friends and connections along the way. You open yourself up to possibilities that may benefit you.

- **It helps you gain confidence**: Stepping out of your comfort zone allows you to take action to accomplish your goals. It makes you believe in your abilities and gain self-confidence. Outside your comfort zone, you'll test yourself more and build up your resilience. As a result, you'll become more successful in life.

Leaving the Comfort Zone to Reach the Growth Zone

In your comfort zone, you have your routines and habits that help you predict your actions and get things done. It's not a bad idea because it assists you in establishing your boundaries, resting when you feel overwhelmed, and reflecting on yourself. However, if you spend all your time there, you can't develop your abilities, and it may get you stuck. You'll finally enter the growth zone when you step out of your comfort zone. You'll improve your current strengths while also learning new experiences and skills. This zone gives you the chance to go on an adventure to self-discovery. You're more curious and willing to take risks.

Tips to Support Stepping Out of Your Comfort Zone

If you want to get out of your comfort zone, chances are it won't be easy because you'll probably have to face some obstacles and endure some pressure. If you push forward, though, you'll discover how beneficial it really is. Here are some tips to help you on your journey to the growth zone:

- **Prioritize what's important**: Sometimes, you might want to stay in your comfort zone by playing on your phone instead of doing your homework. However, it's not good because you know that your homework is due the next day. This is why it's important to set priorities rather than becoming too cozy and ending up worsening your grades at school.

- **Take small steps**: When you set goals to go beyond your comfort zone, it's crucial to start small. Even if you make slow progress, continuing is better than giving up. When you start big, you might feel overwhelmed and decide to stop because you can't handle it.
- **Reframe your stress**: In Chapter 3, I explained that not all stress is harmful because it can be exciting and fun, too, like eustress. When you feel stressed out, you may shift your mind to label it as positive. This way, you can use your stress to motivate yourself to reach your goals.

Methods to Step Outside Your Comfort Zone

You grow when you leave your comfort zone. This is why you must try to get beyond it as much as you can. The following are several ways to do it:

- **Learn to tolerate discomfort**: Expanding your comfort zone is one method to step outside of it. You shouldn't run away when you feel discomfort. For instance, you're invited to meet your parents' friends. If you feel panicked, you should try to stay as long as you can. It'll start to feel more comfortable after a while and with sufficient practice.

- **Spend time with accomplished individuals**: If you want to reach your goals, it's important to hang out with those who have already accomplished them. Their influence will eventually begin to have an impact on your actions. For example, if you want to get better grades in your math class, you should hang out with kids who are good at math.

- **Clearly define the issue you want to resolve**: You should make a list of your discomforts. Keep in mind that fear is the main feeling you're attempting to get rid of. In social settings, are you hesitant to approach people and introduce yourself? Why? Do you fear being ignored? Or are you scared they might judge your appearance? Get specific with your fears so that you can face them head-on.

- **Change your routine**: When you have a routine, it's easy to always follow it because it gives you consistency and aids in getting things done. However, when you're too focused on your routine, you may feel like you're running on autopilot. This is why you need to break out of that by changing your routine. For instance, let's say you always do your homework at home in your room. You could change your routine by doing it at a café or a friend's house.

SEEKING YOUR PEOPLE

In Chapter 7, we talked about how crucial it is to establish a network of friends and family since you'll have people who care about you, gain self-confidence, and become more self-aware. However, there are even more benefits that you may get from strong social support.

The first one is dealing with stress. When you have social support, you'll become better at managing your stress. If you're surrounded by supportive friends and family, you'll feel happier and more content with life. Even if you're faced with obstacles, you can rely on them to guide you to find solutions. Additionally, strong social support also develops your motivation. When you have goals, you can stay on track and keep yourself motivated with the help of your loved ones. For example, if you're trying to lose weight, you can connect with people at the gym who have the same goal and work out together. Lastly, social support will lead you to make better and healthier choices. Your loved one can encourage you to start a healthy diet, avoid alcohol, or study more. This is why having positive individuals on your side can make all the difference.

The Difference Between Social Support and Social Integration

Your social environment influences your well-being as well as your overall health. Your social world is divided into two parts, which are social support and social integration. Social support involves resources offered by social networks to help you deal with stress (Cherry, 2023b). It may take a variety of shapes, such as offering monetary support when someone needs it, providing emotional support when your friend is going through a breakup, or caring for a sick loved one. Meanwhile, social integration is your demonstrated participation in social ties (Yadav, 2023). These social ties include family, friendships, romantic relationships, and religious community.

Types of Social Support

Social support may come in various ways and have different functions for you. The four main categories of social support are as follows (Scott, 2020):

- **Emotional**: This type of support can be given through offering physical comfort, listening, and empathizing with someone. Maybe your mom is going through a difficult time at her workplace, and you hug her and listen to her issues.

- **Informational**: This type of support is expressed by sharing information and giving advice to solve an issue. For instance, your best friend wants to get better grades, and you may advise them to get tutoring sessions.
- **Esteem**: This is demonstrated through giving encouragement and motivation. For example, suppose you were rejected by your crush. In that case, your friend might use esteem support by pointing out your strengths and reminding you that you can always get a better boyfriend later.
- **Tangible**: This happens by taking actions to help someone manage their issues. Maybe your dad is sick, and you decide to cook him breakfast so that he can rest.

How Your Social Support Helps You Leave Your Comfort Zone and Achieve Goals

Your friends, family members, and communities can be people you may depend on to help you step out of your comfort zone and finally accomplish your goals. They'll provide you with ways to realize your potential. From Troy and Gabriella's story, it can be seen how they supported each other for the audition callback. They also used their friends' help to assist them in preparing for it. Without each other's collaboration, they knew that they could never get chosen for the school musical. The people around you, your communities, and their acceptance will motivate you to take on more challenges and reach your goals.

NO SUCH THING AS OVERNIGHT SUCCESS

We've all failed at something in life, and there's nobody in this world who can be perfect at everything the first time they try. Failure is inevitable because it's part of the process of achieving success. You might've gotten bad grades, failed a test, or had a fight with your best friend. No matter what it is, you shouldn't give up. The critical thing to remember is to learn from every setback. I know that failure can be painful, and it doesn't make you feel good. You may think that you can never get back up or come back from it, but that's not true at all. Failure isn't easy to accept, especially if you've given your all. However, you should begin to accept that failures will happen from time to time along the way, and what you can do is move forward every time.

How Learning From Failures Helps You Realign and Refocus

When you fail, it means that you didn't achieve your goal. Most often, it brings you back to the start of the journey. From this point, you can look back at the entire process. You then realize that you can't take the same method to achieve the goal so that you don't end up with failure again. Therefore, failing inspires new ideas for overcoming challenges. You'll realign your ideas and focus on other ways to accomplish what you want. For example, if you failed to land a part-time job, you should look back at the interview session and search for ways you could improve. This means that you can prepare better for your next application.

How Failures Help You Discover Your Strengths and Weaknesses

Failure will make you reflect on yourself. When you don't introspect yourself, you can never know what you're good or bad at. After you fail, you must take some time to process it. What went well? What went wrong? Where exactly did things go wrong? You can use failure to assess where you went wrong, how you can tweak and improve how you go about things, or even change your entire direction. For instance, if you failed to get a high score on your S.A.T., you might analyze your results and find that your score on the writing test was high but that you did poorly in the math section. This means that you should focus more on studying math for your next test.

How Failures Help You Become More Confident

I've mentioned that you must learn from failure to move forward in life. Perhaps you're one of those people who become more determined when someone says that you can't do something. This means that you want to prove them wrong. Failure can be a good teacher that motivates you to be more confident in your abilities. Let's say you're practicing your communication skills. You start by talking more with your classmates or strangers, but you experience failures sometimes because you get easily panicked and nervous. However, you don't stop trying, no matter how difficult it gets. After several months, you become comfortable conversing with others, even if they're strangers. When you see progress, your self-confidence improves. It fuels your motivation and helps you believe you can achieve your goals.

What Lessons Can You Learn from Failures?

Many things can be learned even when you fail. Would you like to start learning from them? Let's explore the lessons you may gain:

- **Creativity**: When you fail, you'll need to find new ideas to overcome the issue and finally achieve your goal. This means that you'll become more creative so that you don't end up with the same result.

- **Flexibility**: Even if you make elaborate plans, something might still go wrong. When failure happens, it forces you to learn how to adapt and be flexible so that the end goal can still be achieved.

- **Motivation**: Your failures can become your motivators. When you fail at something and see someone else succeed, you'll want to prove that you can do the same. This will give you the push to try again after failing.

How to Accept and Learn from Failures

As you grow up, you'll experience different failures. As you pursue your goals, you'll fail at one thing or another. However, they shouldn't stop you from becoming successful. When you fail, you must learn from your mistakes. After a failure, you need to take a step back to organize your mind and find out what went wrong. This way, you'll become more willing to learn from it. The following are some ways to accept and learn from your failures:

- **Find the source of your failures**: Every successful person has failed in their life before. The first step in conquering challenges and achieving success is to learn from your failures. When you fail, think about what went wrong. Was it a direct outcome of your actions? Or was there an external force that caused it? When you fail a test because you didn't study hard enough, don't be scared to take accountability. You should reflect on your actions and change your ways next time.

- **Accept change**: Failure is when your desired outcome doesn't happen as planned. This means that you need to reorganize and change your plan. It's understandable why some dislike change so much because they enjoy their plans and routines. If you want to learn from failures, you must embrace the change and accept that not everything will go the way you want it to. For instance, you planned to get into the basketball team but failed to do so. Instead of getting depressed, you need to review your plan and analyze what your mistakes were; once you figure them out, you may then create a different plan.

- **Sort your ideas**: Not all ideas that you think of will be good. When your mind likes working, you'll want to apply every idea that appears. You need to slow down. You should write down all these ideas and filter them. For example, you're thinking of making your presentation to be more exciting. Maybe your ideas are wearing a costume, bringing a poster, or making a colourful PowerPoint. Before acting on these ideas, you need to understand your audience and the situation. Once you understand them, you may choose the appropriate ideas and run with them.

KEY TAKEAWAYS

- A comfort zone is a space where you feel safe and in control.
- You'll feel afraid when leaving your comfort zone because the outside world is uncertain.
- Several benefits of leaving your comfort zone include making you stronger, meeting new people, gaining positive experiences, and growing your confidence.
- When you leave your comfort zone, you'll reach the growth zone.
- To support yourself in leaving your comfort zone, you should start prioritizing, taking small steps, and reframing stress.
- Some methods to step out of your comfort zone are learning to tolerate discomfort, spending time with accomplished individuals,

and clearly defining the issue you want to resolve.

- Strong social support will help you manage stress, face obstacles, develop motivation, and make healthier choices.
- Social support involves input from your loved ones that helps you handle stress, and social integration means participation in social groups.
- The four types of social support are emotional support, informational support, esteem support, and tangible support.
- Social support helps you leave your comfort zone and accomplish goals.
- Learning from failures is crucial because it helps you realign and refocus, discover your strengths and weaknesses, and become more confident.
- A few ways you might grow through failure are by becoming more creative, more flexible, and more motivated.
- To accept and learn from failures, you must find their sources, accept change, and sort your ideas.

To boost your self-confidence, you must start by improving your self-esteem and self-awareness, as explained in Chapter 1. After that, you should practice positive self-talk and stop pitying yourself to create a healthy self-concept, as you've learned in Chapter 2. In Chapter 3, you learned to recognize your stress and find coping mechanisms to handle it. Additionally, excessive social media use can affect your self-confidence negatively, so you must reduce your screen time and find ways to utilize it to your advantage, as mentioned in Chapter 4. In the next chapter, you discovered how important it is to have a growth mindset, let go of perfectionism, and develop resilience. I've also explained that it is essential not to give in to peer pressure, to set personal boundaries, and to set goals in Chapter 6. In Chapter 7, you found out that teenagers often suffer from mood swings because of various changes. This is why you need to learn how to manage your emotions and tell others how you're feeling. In this chapter, we covered how crucial it is to leave your comfort zone, no matter how scary it is, and learn from your failures.

The lessons you've learned from this book are there to boost your self-confidence, and I hope that you feel more prepared to navigate your teenage years. The B.E.S.T. methods I've explained in this book will help you become confident in who you are as you work on being the best version of yourself. Even when things get rough, keep going because you can become confident when you put in the effort!

SPREADING CONFIDENCE

Now that you have everything you need to build unshakeable self-confidence, it's time to pass on your newfound knowledge and show other readers where they can find the same help.

Simply by leaving your honest opinion of this book on Amazon, you'll show other teens where they can find the information they're looking for and pass their passion for self-confidence forward.

Thank you for your help. The journey to self-confidence is kept alive when we pass on our knowledge – and you're helping me to do just that.

Scan the QR code below to leave your review:

You've arrived at the end of this book. How do you feel about completing it? Do you feel proud of yourself? Were you confident you could finish it? You've learned all the strategies you need to improve your self-confidence while also getting rid of self-doubt and self-limiting beliefs. You have the knowledge and tips from this book to apply in your day-to-day life. The key is to keep practicing these tips and start with small steps first. Are you prepared to stand up and begin executing your first move?

This book has taught you how important it is to be confident in your success because, with it, you'll reach your dreams. Under the Be Curious section, you learned that having healthy self-esteem is essential for your growth as a teenager because poor self-esteem will lead to poor self-confidence. Remember, you also need to be self-aware in order to understand your needs and build relationships. You need to talk to yourself positively if you want to build confidence in yourself. When your self-talk is negative, your mind is filled with bad thoughts that don't allow you to move forward. You also have to stop pitying yourself; self-pity can become an addiction that makes you dwell on your misfortunes. Moreover, your reality is a result of your thoughts. Your experiences in life create your self-concept, and you get to lead it to become positive or negative. In Chapter 3, you discover that experiencing stress from time to time is normal and that stress can be a good motivator too. However, if you feel like it's getting too overwhelming, you must use healthy coping mechanisms and seek help from others.

In the Embrace Possibilities section, you begin by understanding that unhealthy social media use can affect your mental health negatively because you're faced with various unrealistic standards. However, you must change how you use social media to take its benefits by reducing your screen time and filtering what content you see and follow. On social media, being authentic and sticking to your true self is important. You need to accept and love yourself rather than try to follow standards you can't meet. After that, you learned that your mindset matters, so you must cultivate a growth mindset instead of a fixed mindset. You have to understand that everyone makes mistakes, so you shouldn't become a perfectionist. Perfectionism may ruin your self-confidence because you're too focused on not making any mistakes. Instead, you need to get back up each time you fail to build your resilience so that you can bounce back when faced with any obstacle.

Under the Seek to Transform section, you learned that during your teenage years, you'll have to face peer pressure. You might want to give in to it to fit in with the crowd, but remember to stay true to yourself. Peer pressure can be positive when it leads you to achieve your goals, but it may also be harmful by asking you to engage in dangerous activities. This is why you must set boundaries so that you don't get pushed around. Your boundaries will help you keep your identity without having to always follow what others want.

Additionally, setting goals is also crucial to keep yourself organized while staying on track to reach success. In Chapter 7, you were faced with the fact that it's normal to have mood swings as a teenager because your life is changing physically, socially, and emotionally. You need to learn how to regulate your emotions because of this. You should learn to tell others how you're really feeling by cultivating communication skills. It's also essential to create a support system that'll help you go through the hardships of life. In the last chapter, you were advised to leave your comfort zone and develop your abilities. It'll be difficult at first because you'll have to face fear and various obstacles, but once you get comfortable with them, you'll find it very rewarding. Social support is crucial here because it'll make leaving your comfort zone much easier. Furthermore, failure is normal. What you should do is learn from it and do better next time.

All the tips and suggestions from this book were the ones I used to overcome my low self-confidence and insecurity. If they worked for me, they would work for you as well. These tips will benefit you in so many ways; not only will they boost your self-confidence, but they'll also help you better your self-esteem, establish stronger relationships, improve your performance at school, decrease self-doubt, and escape from self-limiting beliefs. Every chapter of this book prepares you to face the obstacles that stop you from going after your goals and helps you to build confidence from the inside out.

It can be tough to be confident, especially when you're still trying to understand who you are—but don't worry! While confidence can take time, each step you need to build the foundations of unstoppable self-confidence is within the pages of this book. You can be confident in who you are regardless of which season in life you are in.

If you find the tips I provided in this book helpful, please leave a review on Amazon!

REFERENCES

Ackerman, C. (2020, April 1). *What is self-awareness? (+5 ways to be more self-aware).* Positive Psychology. https://positivepsychology.com/self-awareness-matters-how-you-can-be-more-self-aware/

Alice. (2020). *Overcoming low self-esteem.* Notes by Alice. https://notesbyalice.co.uk/overcoming-low-self-esteem/

Allan, A. (2022, September 26). *Mental health: Warning signs and when to ask for help.* UNICEF. https://www.unicef.org/jordan/stories/mental-health-warning-signs-and-when-ask-help

Bailey, A. (2022, October 18). *Coping mechanisms: Everything you need to know.* Very Well Health. https://www.verywellhealth.com/coping-mechanisms-5272135

Beck, J. S. (2011). *Cognitive behavior therapy: Basics and beyond.* (2nd Edition). Guilford Press.

Bernstein, J. (2011, October 23). *Climbing off the slippery slope of self-pity.* Psychology Today. https://www.psychologytoday.com/intl/blog/liking-the-child-you-love/201110/climbing-the-slippery-slope-self-pity

Betz, M. (2022, September 14). *What is self-awareness and why is it important?* Better Up. https://www.betterup.com/blog/what-is-self-awareness

Break your maladaptive coping patterns with five effective techniques. (2023, January 1). Life Recovery. https://www.djburr.com/blog/break-your-maladaptive-coping-patterns-with-five-effective-techniques

Campbell, L. (2023, April 26). *Why personal boundaries are important and how to set them.* Psych Central. https://psychcentral.com/relationships/what-are-personal-boundaries-how-do-i-get-some

Cassata, C. (2021, September 25). *8 ways to accept yourself.* Psych

Central. https://psychcentral.com/lib/ways-to-accept-your-self#how-to-accept-yourself

Cherney, K. (2020, August 6). *What is social media addiction?* Healthline. https://www.healthline.com/health/social-media-addiction#decreasing-use

Cherry, K. (2022a, July 22). *5 reasons emotions are important.* Very Well Mind. https://www.verywellmind.com/the-purpose-of-emotions-2795181

Cherry, K. (2022b, November 7). *What is self-concept?* Very Well Mind. https://www.verywellmind.com/what-is-self-concept-2795865

Cherry, K. (2022c, November 7). *What is self-esteem?* Very Well Mind. https://www.verywellmind.com/what-is-self-esteem-2795868

Cherry, K. (2022d, October 6). *10 ways to build resilience.* Very Well Mind. https://www.verywellmind.com/ways-to-become-more-resilient-2795063

Cherry, K. (2022e, September 20). *What is a mindset and why it matters?* Very Well Mind. https://www.verywellmind.com/what-is-a-mindset-2795025#citation-2

Cherry, K. (2023a, February 13). *11 signs of self-esteem.* Very Well Mind. https://www.verywellmind.com/signs-of-low-self-esteem-5185978

Cherry, K. (2023b, March 3). *How social support contributes to psychological health.* Very Well Mind. https://www.verywellmind.com/social-support-for-psychological-health-4119970#citation-3

Cooks-Campbell, A. (2022, February 22). *Coping mechanisms: Definition and how they function.* Better Up. https://www.betterup.com/blog/coping-mechanisms

Crevin, M. (2020, July 14). *8 ways teens can improve their communication skills.* Your Teen Mag. https://yourteenmag.com/family-life/communication/ways-to-improve-communication

Davis, T. (2023). *Mindsets: Definition, examples, and books (growth, fixed + other types.* Berkeley Well Being. https://www.berkeleywellbeing.com/mindsets.html

DeJong, C. (2020, August 2020). *7 ways self-pity impacts addiction and why gratitude matters in recovery.* Carrie DeJong. https://www.car-riedejong.com/blog/self-pity-and-substance-use

Du, H., King, R. B., & Chi, P. (2017). Self-esteem and subjective well-being revisited: The roles of personal, relational, and collective self-esteem. *PLOS ONE,* 12(8).

Dweck, C. S. (2007). *Mindset: The new psychology of success.* Ballantine Books.

Eberly, L. (2022, November 16). *A deep dive into Anti-Hero by Taylor Swift.* Valkyrie. https://wshsvalkyrie.com/2316/art-and-style/a-deep-dive-into-anti-hero-by-taylor-swift/

Elizabeth, A. (2022, September 26). *What is resilience and why is it important for success?* Life Hack. https://www.life-hack.org/715558/what-is-resilience-and-how-to-be-resilient

George, C. (2021, April 19). *10 ways to step out of your comfort zone and overcome your fear.* Life Hack. https://www.lifehack.org/arti-cles/communication/10-ways-step-out-your-comfort-zone-and-enjoy-taking-risks.html

Gillette, H. (2021, September 7). *How to recognize and redirect self-pity.* Psych Central. https://psychcentral.com/blog/self-pity-to-self-compassion#why-to-avoid-self-pity

Gillette, H. (2022, April 12). *The makeup and theories of self-concept.* Psych Central. https://psychcentral.com/health/self-concept#self-concept-theories

Goldstein, J. M., Seidman, L. J., Horton, N. J., Makris, N., Kennedy, D. N., Caviness, V. S., Faraone, S. V., & Tsuang, M. T. (2001). Normal sexual dimorphism of the adult human brain assessed by in vivo magnetic resonance imaging. *Cerebral Cortex, 11*(6), 490-497.

Goleman, D. (2000). *Emotional intelligence: Issues in paradigm building.* Consortium for Research on Emotional Intelligence in Organizations. https://www.eiconsortium.org/reprints/ei_is-sues_in_paradigm_building.html

Griffin, T. (2022, March 9). *How to learn from your failures: 4 valuable lessons.* Business. https://www.business.com/articles/learning-from-failure/

Hailey, L. (2023). *How to set boundaries: 5 ways to draw the line politely.* Science of People. https://www.scienceofpeople.com/how-to-set-boundaries/

Hampton, D. (2018, February 25). *How setting goals can help and hurt your mental health.* The Best Brain Possible. https://thebestbrain-possible.com/goals-mental-health-brain-habits/

Harm, M. (2023, May 3). *Lizzo's best tips for improving body confidence.* The Every Girl. https://theeverygirl.com/lizzo-self-love-summer-tips/

Heitz, D. (2017, December 24). *Perfectionism.* Healthline. https://www.healthline.com/health/perfectionism#symptoms

Herrity, J. (2023, July 10). *How to write SMART goals in 5 steps (with examples).* Indeed. https://www.indeed.com/career-advice/career-development/how-to-write-smart-goals

Ho, L. (2023, June 5). *What is goal setting and why is it so important?* Life Hack. https://www.lifehack.org/articles/lifestyle/goal-setting-the-why-behind-the-what.html

Hodge, K. (2023, June 14). *12 healthy coping mechanisms: Unlocking inner strength.* Mental Health Center. https://www.mentalhealth-center.org/healthy-coping-mechanisms/

Holland, K. (2020, June 27). *Positive self-talk: How talking to yourself is a good thing.* Healthline. https://www.healthline.com/health/posi-tive-self-talk#examples-of-positive-self--talk

Hosogi, M., Okada, A., Fujii, C., Noguchi, K., & Watanabe, K. (2012). Importance and usefulness of evaluating self-esteem in children. *BioPsychoMedicine,* (9).

How can I improve myself? (2023). Mind. https://www.mind.org.uk/in-formation-support/types-of-mental-health-problems/self-esteem/tips-to-improve-your-self-esteem/

How setting goals can positively impact our mental health. (2023). Center Stone. https://centerstone.org/our-resources/health-well ness/how-setting-goals-can-positively-impact-our-mental-health/

Importance of goal setting. (2023, July 17). Success Starts Within.

https://www.successstartswithin.com/blog/importance-of-goal-setting

Incongruence. (2023). Alley Dog. https://www.alleydog.com/glossary/definition.php?term=Incongruence

Jacobson, R. (2022, September 2). *Social media and self-doubt.* Child Mind. https://childmind.org/article/social-media-and-self-doubt/

Journaling with teens. (n.d.). The University of Missouri. https://extension.missouri.edu/publications/gh6150

Kerlinger, C. (2022, October 22). *Lizzo: The plus-size feminist artist taking the music industry by storm. Ben* Vaughn. https://www.ben-vaughn.com/lizzo-the-plus-size-feminist-artist-taking-the-music-industry-by-storm/

Lindsey. (n.d.). *How do emotions affect our bodies?* SLO Health Center. https://www.slohealthcenter.com/how-do-emotions-affect-our-body/

Lonczak, H. (2020, July 24). *Increase client's self-love: 26 exercises & worksheets.* Positive Psychology. https://positivepsychology.com/self-love-exercises-worksheets/

Lyons, M. (2021, September 7). *Being your authentic self is easier said than done but worth it.* Better Up. https://www.betterup.com/blog/authentic-self

Maddock, S. (2023). *What causes stress? Internal and external stressors.* Well Professor. https://www.wellprofessor.com/blog/stress-less/what-causes-stress-internal-and-external-stressors

Martin, S. (2018, April 24). *What are boundaries and why do I need them?* Live Well With Sharon Martin. https://www.livewellwithsharonmartin.com/what-are-boundaries/

Martin, S. (2020, April 23). *7 types of boundaries you may need.* Psych Central. https://psychcentral.com/blog/imperfect/2020/04/7-types-of-boundaries-you-may-need#2)-Sexual-Boundaries

Mean girls plot. (n.d.). IMDb. https://www.imdb.com/title/tt0377092/plotsummary/

Meg's story: Body image and self-esteem. (2022, February 14). Gold

Digger Trust. https://www.golddiggertrust.-co.uk/news/2022/1/25/megs-story-body-image-and-self-esteem

Miles, M. (2022, March 30). *Why learning from failure is your key to success.* Better Up. https://www.betterup.com/blog/learning-from-failure

Morgan. (2016, October 20). *Analyzing poetry -Nobody's Perfect by Hannah Montana.* My River Side. http://myriverside.sd43.bc.-ca/morgany2015/2016/10/20/analyzing-poetry-nobodys-perfect-by-hannah-montana/

Morin, A. (2021, September 1). *Ask a therapist: How can I improve my self-esteem?* Very Well Mind. https://www.verywellmind.com/ask-a-therapist-how-can-i-improve-my-self-esteem-5095001

Morin, A. (2022, September 1). *What is peer pressure?* Very Well Family. https://www.verywellfamily.com/negative-and-positive-peer-pressure-differences-2606643

Morris, S. Y. (2016, December 16). *What are the benefits of self-talk?* Healthline. https://www.healthline.com/health/mental-health/self-talk#how-does-it-work

Moulder, H. (n.d.). how to set goals for building self-confidence and fulfillment. Course Correction Coaching. https://www.coursec-orrectioncoaching.com/how-to-set-goals-for-building-self-confi-dence-and-fulfillment/

Neenan, M. (2018). Developing resilience: A cognitive-behavioural approach. Routledge.

O'Shea, D. (2020). *You are not an island.* Debra O'Shea. https://www.-droshea.com/blog/you-are-not-an-island

Page, O. (2020, November 4). *How to leave your comfort zone and enter your growth zone.* Positive Psychology. https://positivepsychology.-com/comfort-zone/#tips

Parent-child relationship – why it's important. (2018, October 25). Parenting NI. https://www.parentingni.org/blog/parent-child-relationship-why-its-important/#:

Patel, S. (2021, November 28). *5 reasons why people are afraid to get out of the comfort zone.* Medium. https://medium.com/the-summit-life/5-reasons-why-people-are-afraid-to-get-out-of-the-comfort-zone-76506c0f4fab

Puff, R. (2017, September 19). *Growth mindset vs. fixed mindset.* Psychology Today. https://www.psychologytoday.com/intl/blog/meditation-modern-life/201709/growth-mindset-vs-fixed-mindset

Raypole, C. (2023, February 9). How to become the boss of your emotions. Healthline. https://www.healthline.com/health/how-to-control-your-emotions#name-it

Rekhi, S. (2023). *Coping mechanisms: Definition, examples, & types.* Berkeley Well-Being. https://www.berkeleywellbeing.com/coping-mechanisms.html

Rice, A. (2021, September 13). *How to challenge negative self-talk.* Psych Central. https://psychcentral.com/lib/challenging-negative-self-talk#takeaway

Richards, P. (2017, June 13). *The importance of belonging in teenagers.* Healthfully. https://healthfully.com/1002787-importance-belonging-teenagers.html

Robinson, L. & Smith, M. (2023, March 29). *Social media and mental health.* Help Guide. https://www.helpguide.org/articles/mental-health/social-media-and-mental-health.htm

Saxena, S. & Sookdeo, T. (2020, December 9). *Peer pressure: Types, examples, & how to respond.* Choosing Therapy. https://www.choosingtherapy.com/peer-pressure/

Scott, E. (2020, November 23). *The different types of social support.* Very Well Mind. https://www.verywellmind.com/types-of-social-support-3144960

Scott, E. (2021, November 7). *What is stress?* Very Well Mind. https://www.verywellmind.com/stress-and-health-3145086

Scott, E. (2022, October 31). *Avoidance coping and why it creates additional stress.* Very Well Mind. https://www.verywellmind.com/avoidance-coping-and-stress-4137836

Scott, E. (2023, February 27). Perfectionism: 10 signs of perfectionist traits. Very Well Mind. https://www.verywellmind.com/signs-you-may-be-a-perfectionist-3145233

Segal, J., Smith, M., & Robinson, L. (2023, April 5). *Stress symptoms, signs, and causes.* Help Guide. https://www.helpguide.org/articles/stress/stress-symptoms-signs-and-causes.htm

Self-esteem and self-confidence. (2023). The University of Queensland. https://my.uq.edu.au/information-and-services/student-support/health-and-wellbeing/self-help-resources/self-esteem-and-self-confidence

Self-talk. (2023). Health Direct. https://www.healthdirect.gov.au/self-talk#:

Setting boundaries. (2021, October 25). WedMD. https://www.web-md.com/mental-health/setting-boundaries

Shafir, H. & Fuller, K. (2022, November 9). *Perfectionism: Signs, causes, & ways to overcome.* Choosing Therapy. https://www.choosingtherapy.com/perfectionism/

Sicinski, A. (2023). *What exactly is a self-concept and how does it impact your life?* Lifetime Achiever. https://blog.iqmatrix.com/self-concept

Sissons, B. (2023, March 1). *How to regain lost self-confidence.* Medical News Today. https://www.medicalnewstoday.com/articles/i-have-lost-my-confidence-and-self-esteem#causes

Social interaction influence on self-esteem from a social psychology perspective. (2022, March 18). Edubirdie. https://edubirdie.com/examples/social-interaction-influence-on-self-esteem-from-a-social-psychology-perspective/

Soken-Huberty, E. (2023). *10 reasons why self-awareness is important.* The Important Site. https://theimportantsite.com/10-reasons-why-self-awareness-is-important/?expand_article=1

Stress. (2021, January 28). Cleveland Clinic. https://my.clevelandclinic.org/health/articles/11874-stress

Sutton, J. (2019, January 3). *What is resilience, and why is it important to bounce back?* Positive Psychology. https://positivepsychology.com/what-is-resilience/

Sutton, J. (2020, October 28). *Maladaptive coping: 15 examples & how to break the cycle*. Positive Psychology. https://positivepsychology.com/maladaptive-coping/

Sutton, J. (2021, October 27). *18 best growth mindset activities, worksheets, and questions*. Positive Psychology. https://positivepsychology.com/growth-mindset/

Tajfel, H. (1982). *Social psychology of intergroup relations. Annual Review of Psychology, 33*, 1-39.

Taylor, M. (2021, August 17). *Perfectionism: 6 consequences to watch for*. WebMD. https://www.webmd.com/balance/features/consequences-perfectionism

The impact of self-talk has on your confidence. (2023, March 29). Success Starts Within. https://www.successstartswithin.com/blog/the-impact-self-talk-has-on-your-confidence

The importance of self-confidence. (2022, October 18). Habitomic. https://habitomic.com/blog/what-is-self-confidence-and-its-importance/

The learning zone model. (2023). Mind Tools. https://www.mindtools.com/a0bop9z/the-learning-zone-model

These celebs talk confidence – from Olivia Rodrigo to Louis Tomlinson. (2021, June 17). Capital FM. https://www.capitalfm.com/lifestyle/celeb-confidence-tips-olivia-rodrigo-louis-tomlinson-zendaya-rihanna/

Understanding confidence and self-esteem. (2023). Mind. https://www.mind.org.uk/for-young-people/feelings-and-experiences/confidence-and-self-esteem/

Valenti, L. (2019, May 30). *5 young celebrities who have opened up about their mental health in 2019*. Vogue. https://www.vogue.com/article/celebrity-mental-health-struggles-justin-bieber-sophie-turner-billie-eilish

Venkataramakrishnan, R. (2018, January 1). *Song for the new year: 'Wait For It' is beautifully distressing lament (but also brings hope)*. Scroll. https://scroll.in/article/863347/song-for-the-new-year-wait-for-it-is-beautifully-distressing-lament-but-also-brings-hope

Vilhauer, J. (2020, September 27). *How your thinking creates your reality*. Psychology Today. https://www.psychologytoday.com/us/blog/living-forward/202009/how-your-thinking-creates-your-reality

Vinney, C. (2018, November 12). *What is self-concept in psychology?* ThoughtCo. https://www.thoughtco.com/self-concept-psychology-4176368

Wahome, C. (2021, August 24). *How to overcome perfectionism*. WebMD. https://www.webmd.com/balance/features/how-to-overcome-perfectionism

What are the 6 types of peer pressure? (2019, November 26). Talk It Out. https://www.talkitoutnc.org/blogs/types-of-peer-pressure/

Why do young women have such low self-esteem? (2022, October 26). Amen Clinics. https://www.amenclinics.com/blog/why-do-young-women-have-such-low-self-esteem/

Why is having a supportive parent is so important for teenagers? (2021, August 27). Academic Heights. https://www.academicheights.in/blog/why-is-having-a-supportive-parent-is-so-important-for-teenagers/#:

Why teens have mood swings: Exploring emotional vulnerability. (2023, February 26). Safes. https://www.safes.so/blogs/why-teenagers-susceptible-to-changing-emotions/

Yadav, S. (2023, June 30). *Social integration: Sociology definition & 10 examples*. Helpful Professor. https://helpfulprofessor.com/social-integration-sociology/

Zimmerman, P. (2023, May 11). *How emotions are made*. Noldus Information Technology. https://www.noldus.com/blog/how-emotions-are-made